The Complete Guide to Lineage Societies:

the Who, What, Where, and How

By Kimberly Ormsby Nagy, AG®

Genealogical Publishing Company

Published by Genealogical Publishing Company
Baltimore, Maryland
2024

ISBN 9780806321394

To my mother –

my first genealogy “buddy”,

with fond memories of cemeteries, courthouses, and microfilm readers.

TABLE OF CONTENTS

PREFACE

This book grew out of my love of lineage societies. There are so many societies in existence today that there is truly something for everyone. And new societies are being formed every year. However, most people may have heard only of the "Colonial Dames" or the "Daughters of the American Revolution" and do not realize there are many other societies out there. Lineage societies also have a reputation of being made up of little old ladies, sitting around in their fancy hats and drinking tea. Yet. there is so much more that lineage societies accomplish. Many have young adults or even children as members. The wide array of types of societies one can join as well as the services they perform is addressed in Chapters 1-4.

After serving as a Registrar for several societies, I realized that compiling an application for a society requires a set of skills that is not taught in most genealogical lectures. While an application requires sound genealogical principles to determine the lineage, there is a difference in the type and quantity of references required, as well as how those references are cited. Compiling applications is addressed in detail in Chapters 5-8.

While this book cannot address every society, several examples are included in the Appendix. A brief description of membership qualifications is included for those societies, along with contact information.

It is my hope that this book helps the reader learn about the variety of societies in existence, as well as all the varied purposes of these societies. I also hope that I can demystify the process of applying for membership so that more people are encouraged to join the society or societies of their choice.

I would like to acknowledge everyone who has encouraged me along my lineage society journey. I have met and worked with so many wonderful people in these societies and many have become lifelong friends.

Special thanks to Shari Worrell for her input, and to Sandy Zeles for her editorial advice.

CHAPTER 1

WHAT IS A LINEAGE SOCIETY?

More than 300 Lineage Societies are active in the United States today. But what exactly is a Lineage Society?

The simple definition is: A Lineage Society is a group of individuals who all descend from a specific group of ancestors.

All of the qualifying ancestors for a given society will have something in common. For example, they may be from a specific immigration event, such as the *Mayflower* passengers.

They may be the founders or first settlers of a colony, town, or state. This may be as early as the Jamestown settlement, or more recent, as in the Daughters of Utah Pioneers.

They may have served in a specific war, such as the Revolutionary War or the War of 1812. Societies such as the Daughters of the American Revolution or the United States Daughters of 1812 recognize not only military service but civil service or patriotic service as well.

Many societies honor ancestors who contributed public service by serving as an elected official, delegate to the General Court, mayor, town clerk, highway surveyor, and so on. This service may be limited to a particular time period such as the Colonial Daughters of the 17th Century (before 1700) or Daughters of the American Colonists (before 1776).

While many societies honor ancestors who were prominent in their community, some will honor the "common man" as well. The Guild of Colonial Artisans and Tradesmen honors ancestors who worked to build their communities, such as blacksmiths, millers, and butchers.

A few societies honor ancestors who arrived in the colonies in the service of another individual. The Descendants of Colonial Indentured Servants seeks to honor those men and women who agreed to servitude in order to secure passage to the colonies. The Sons and Daughters of the U.S. Middle Passage honors those ancestors who had no choice but were forced into slavery.

Some societies honor ancestors with a specific occupation or profession, such as Colonial Clergy, Descendants of Early Postmasters, or Descendants of Textile workers.

Other societies honor ancestors who practiced a specific religion, such as Descendants of Early Quakers or the National Huguenot Society.

A few societies honor specific groups of ancestors. These include the Associated Daughters of Early American Witches which honors those people who were suspected, accused, or tried for witchcraft in the colonies during the seventeenth century.

The Descendants of Colonial Regulators honors ancestors who fought against taxation without representation in colonial America. The Southern Dames of America honors ancestors from the southern states.

Some societies honor descent from old-world royalty. One example is the Order of the Red Dragon (Welsh Kings). Some old-world societies honor descent from a specific Royal such as Lady Godiva or St. Margaret of Scotland.

Lineage Societies are also known as Hereditary Societies because members must prove their descent from the specific ancestors of that society.

However, a Lineage Society should not be confused with a Heritage Society which honors a specific cultural heritage and does not require proof of lineage from specific ancestors. An example of a Heritage Society might be the local German American Society or an Italian American Social Club.

Members join a Lineage Society for a variety of reasons. They may wish to prove their descent from a particular individual and have it preserved for future generations. By joining, they are honoring their ancestor and their memory.

The process of applying and being approved allows the individual's research to be vetted and approved by another person or committee, lending credibility to that research.

Members may join because they believe in the society's mission – they may want to get involved in the historic preservation or patriotic activities of a certain society. More about society missions in Chapter 2.

Many members join for the sense of community and connections with like-minded people in that organization. They feel a type of kinship with other members due to their shared lineage.

Figure 1 – Sons of the American Revolution Color Guard.

The majority of lineage societies require direct descent from a qualifying ancestor. In other words, a grandparent, great-grandparent, etc. A few societies allow collateral descent as well. This is usually limited to a sibling of a grandparent or great-grandparent, and so on. For example, because so many young men who served in the Civil War did not survive to have descendants, the National Society Daughters of the Union and the United Daughters of the Confederacy honor those ancestors through descendants of their siblings.

Because these societies are based on hereditary descent, most do not allow adoptees to join, unless they can prove descent through a biological parent. With the advent of DNA, more adoptees are able to document biological lineage and societies are beginning to accept DNA evidence as proof of eligibility.

While most lineage societies are based on descent from an ancestor several generations removed, there are a few that honor more modern or twentieth-century ancestors. The Descendants of American Farmers honors ancestors who farmed prior to 1914. The members of the Military Order of the Southern Cross of the Pacific Theater have ancestors who served between 1941 and 1951. The Descendants of American Prisoners of War includes ancestors up to the present day.

There are lineage societies based in other countries besides the United States, however, they are outside the scope of this book. Some of the larger U.S.-based societies may have overseas chapters, such as the Daughters of the American Revolution or the Mayflower Society.

CHAPTER 2

WHAT DOES A LINEAGE SOCIETY DO?

Each of the more than 300 lineage societies in the United States today has its own unique purpose. Those purposes or missions can be sorted into several categories.

Above all, the mission of each society is to honor a group of ancestors and establish a record of their lineage.

Some of the varied missions can be categorized as Historic Preservation, Charitable, Educational, and Patriotic.

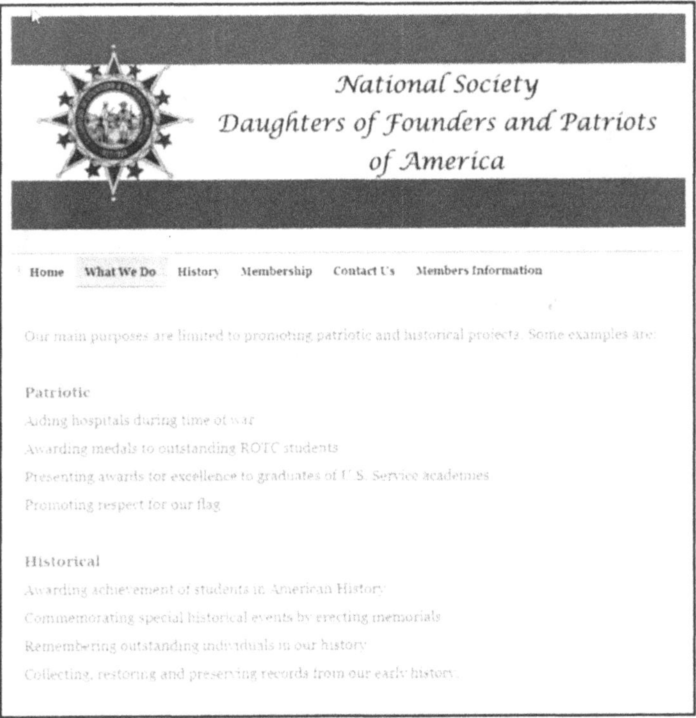

Figure 2.1 – Society purposes from nationalsocietydfpa.com.

Historic Preservation can take many forms. Many societies engage in the preservation of the history of a certain location. This is often done through markings of historic properties or sites.

Grave marking is a form of historic preservation – for example, the marking of a grave of a Revolutionary War soldier, War of 1812 soldier, or Civil War soldier. Other individuals may be marked as well, such as "Real Daughters" – the daughter of a soldier.

Figure 2.2 – Dedication and grave marking of an 1812 patriot.

Historic preservation may extend to archival preservation and digitizing of documents. The Daughters of Founders and Patriots of America has given grants to help preserve documents of the colonial period.

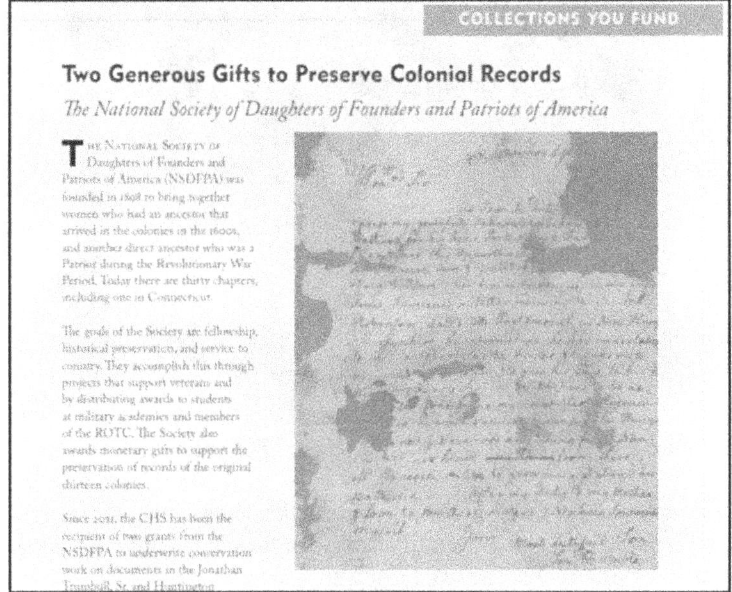

COLLECTIONS YOU FUND

Two Generous Gifts to Preserve Colonial Records

The National Society of Daughters of Founders and Patriots of America

The National Society of Daughters of Founders and Patriots of America (NSDFPA) was founded in 1898 to bring together women who had an ancestor that arrived in the colonies in the 1600s, and another direct ancestor who was a Patriot during the Revolutionary War Period. Today there are thirty chapters, including one in Connecticut.

The goals of the Society are fellowship, historical preservation, and service to country. They accomplish this through projects that support veterans and by distributing awards to students at military academies and members of the ROTC. The Society also awards monetary gifts to support the preservation of records of the original thirteen colonies.

Since 2011, the CHS has been the recipient of two grants from the NSDFPA to underwrite conservation work on documents in the Jonathan Trumbull, Sr. and Huntington

Figure 2.3 – Historic Preservation of Documents.

Preservation of genealogical records is another form of historic preservation. The Daughters of the American Revolution encourages chapters to publish transcriptions of local records or cemetery readings. Several societies publish Lineage Books containing abstracted information from members' applications, which is another way to preserve genealogical records.

Education is another common mission of lineage societies. This too may take several forms. Some societies encourage members to help educate our youth about historic events.

Many societies offer scholarships to high school and college students. These scholarships may reflect the membership requirements of the society itself. For example, The National Society Descendants of American Farmers offers scholarships to students pursuing degrees in Agriculture. The Guild of Colonial Artisans and Tradesmen has an endowment at the American College of the Building Arts in South Carolina that supports students learning traditional building trades.

Figure 2.4 – Awarding a Colonial Dames 17th Century Scholarship.

Societies that have children as members are active in educating those children in history, patriotism, and aspects of leadership, including public speaking and parliamentary procedure. The two most well-known societies for children are the Children of the American Revolution and the Children of the American Colonists. A few societies recognize children as "junior" members along with adult members, such as the US Daughters of 1812 and the Women Descendants of the Ancient and Honorable Artillery Company.

Figure 2.5 – Children of the American Colonists learning history.

Fostering patriotism is another purpose of some societies. Members may be encouraged to assist with the tutoring of immigrants in preparation for their citizenship examinations. DAR offers awards for Good Citizenship for high school seniors and encourages service work in the community.

Several societies provide awards to military students. They may be in JROTC or ROTC programs. Some also present awards to students in Military Academies.

Figure 2.6 – Coast Guard Academy Cadet receiving a society award.

Support of the military may include sending care packages or greeting cards to deployed service personnel, assisting families of deployed service members, and similar activities.

Patriotic support extends to the care of veterans. This may take the form of assistance at Veterans Homes or Hospitals. Donations to agencies serving homeless veterans are a popular activity. Other agencies that support veterans also benefit from lineage society support; one popular type of recipient are the agencies that support disabled veterans or those suffering from Post-Traumatic Stress Disorder by providing service animals.

Figure 2.7 – Children of the American Revolution honors their members who serve in the military.

Most societies have some form of charitable mission. In addition to support of veterans, other charities may benefit. The Southern Dames of America is passionate about support for vision care. This ranges from simply encouraging members to recycle their eyeglasses to monetary support of schools for the blind, grants for research in vision care, and donations of braille materials.

Figure 2.8 – Southern Dames of America donating money for eye research.

This is just a small sampling of the various missions of lineage societies. Each has its own set of purposes. Prospective members are encouraged to learn more about any mission that appeals to them.

CHAPTER 3

HOW TO LOCATE A LINEAGE SOCIETY

There are many ways to locate a lineage society of interest. The easiest way is simply to search for a specific society in your web browser. Searching using terms such as “Descendants” or “First Families” may also help.

The best online listing for most lineage societies is at hereditary.us. This site is maintained by the Hereditary Society Community and contains information about numerous societies, including basic eligibility information and how to contact them. Hereditary.us also lists some meeting dates as well as other items of interest relating to lineage societies; however, some of the newest societies are not listed yet.

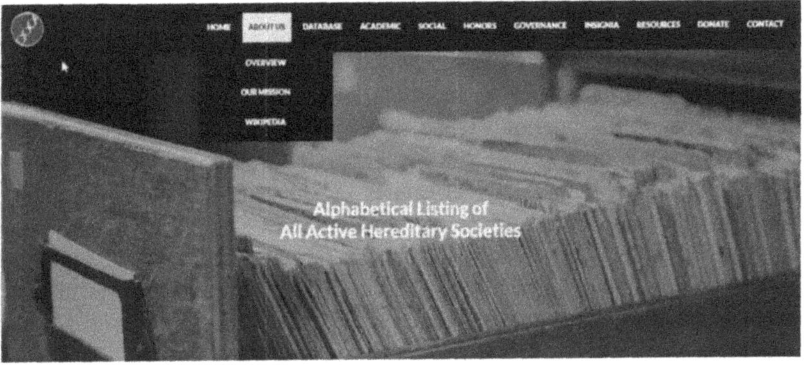

Figure 3.1 – hereditary.us lists most active lineage societies.

Cyndi’s list at cyndislist.com is another resource for finding many lineage societies, although it is not nearly as complete as the Hereditary Society Community site.

The Appendix in this book has basic information for several societies that are mentioned in these pages.

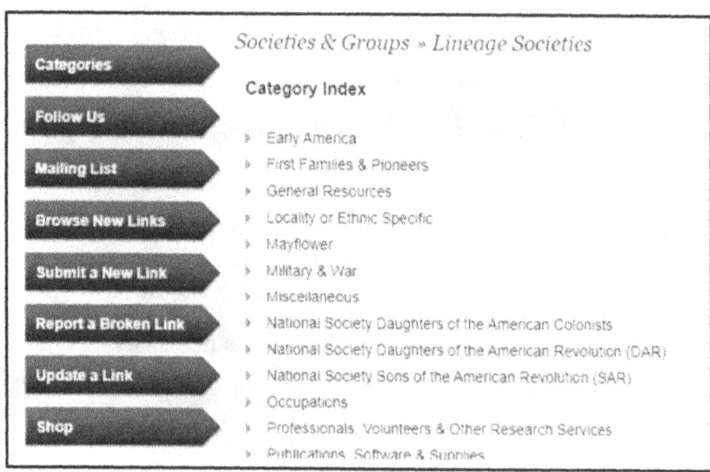

Figure 3.2 – Categories of Lineage Societies at cyndislist.com.

Most lineage societies have a webpage with information about their objectives, their officers, listings of eligible ancestors, and either an email or a contact form to request more information. If the society is organized into state and local chapters, there is often a way to contact them, as well as the national society itself. For example, the Colonial Dames 17th Century website has a contact form which asks visitors to enter their city and state of residence. That information is then forwarded to the chapter closest to them. The Sons of the American Revolution website contact form will direct prospective members to the state president where they live, and the Daughters of Indian Wars lists email addresses for every state president.

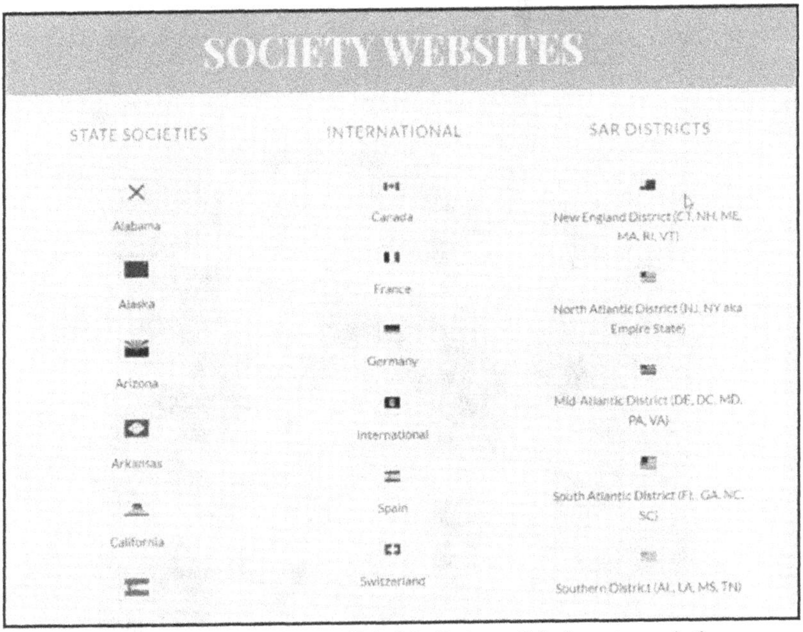

Figure 3.3 – sar.org has a clickable listing of their state societies.

Searching Facebook and other social media sites is another way to find lineage societies. There, one can view posts from society members to get a sense of their activities. A few societies have only a social media presence and no webpage.

Of course, there are offline ways to locate a lineage society as well, especially for local chapters. Local newspapers may have a calendar or notice section for upcoming meetings of various clubs and organizations. They may also publish articles about charitable events and activities by the local chapter.

Some libraries have notices on a community bulletin board for upcoming meetings. Some local chapters of the Daughters of the American Revolution may have scheduled times at the library for assistance with genealogy. Attending one of these sessions is a good way to meet local members as well as gain help with a membership application.

Local genealogical societies may know of lineage groups in their area. In fact, they may have members in some of them. Often, there are brochures from lineage societies at the genealogical society's meeting or conference.

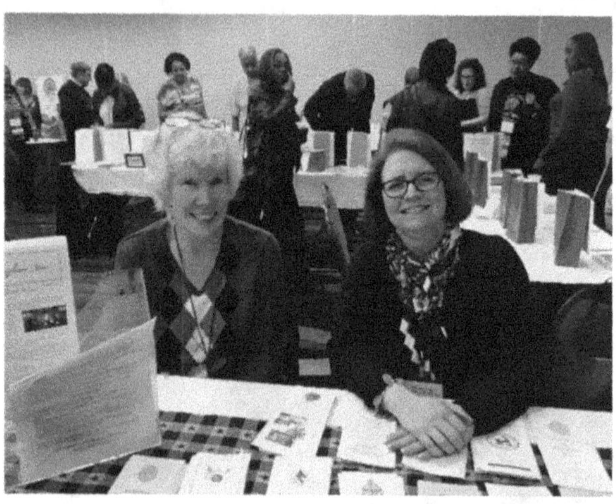

Figure 3.4 – Society representatives with brochures at the Illinois State Genealogical Conference.

Word of mouth is another tried and true way to learn about societies. Once you meet a member of a lineage society, ask if they know members in other societies for which you may qualify.

CHAPTER 4

ELIGIBILITY

There are two main considerations when determining eligibility for a lineage society: lineage and service.

First, can you document your lineage back to the qualifying ancestor? This will be discussed in greater detail in Chapter 6.

Next, does the ancestor's service qualify? Service, defined broadly, can take many forms depending on the society of interest. For societies that honor ancestral service during a war, it can be defined as specific service in the military.

Many societies include other "civil" or "patriotic" services during a conflict as well. For example, the Daughters of the American Revolution considers several categories of service during the Revolutionary War. Military service consists of membership in the army, navy, or militia. DAR also accepts ancestors who participated in civil service. This is defined as service to the state or local government, such as Town Clerk, Highway Surveyor, or Justice of the Peace. Ancestors who provided patriotic service by paying supply tax, supplying goods to the army, or signing an Oath of Allegiance also qualify. The Sons of the American Revolution has a similar list of qualifying service, however, the Sons of the Revolution honors only ancestors who provided military service.

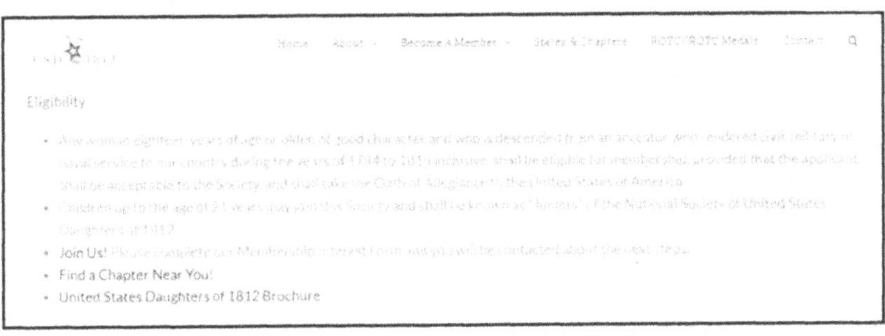

Figure 4.1 – usdaughters1812.org lists general eligibility criteria along with links for membership information.

It is important to read the qualifications for ancestral service for each society. The United States Daughters of 1812 honors ancestors who provided military, civil, and patriotic service during the War of 1812. In addition, service leading up to the actual war qualifies. Any service from 1784 to 1815 is included, such as frontier skirmishes of that era, as well as the War of 1812 itself.

Some societies accept service from more than one military conflict, which may be military or civil. For example, the Daughters of Colonial Wars accepts service throughout the period 1607 to 1775, which includes conflicts from the Pequot War to the French and Indian War. The Daughters of Indian Wars extends the time period to 1900, which also includes several conflicts with Native Americans on the frontier.

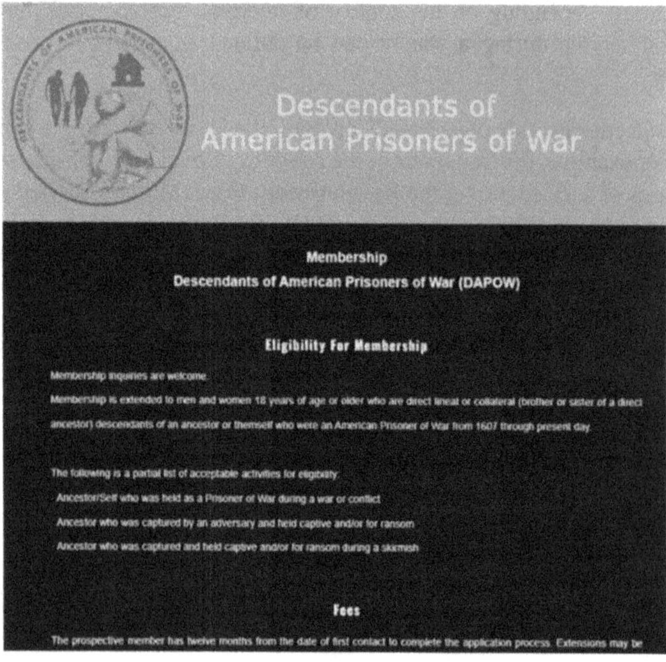

Figure 4.2 – dapow.weebly.com listing of eligibility for membership.

"Service" may be non-military as well. Societies that honor colonial ancestors honor those who contributed to the foundation of this country. The Daughters of American Colonists, the Sons of American Colonists, and the Children of American Colonists, each have 27 categories of "service" for ancestors prior to July 4, 1776. This service may have been military but also includes ministers, physicians, original landowners, and participants in colonial or local government. The service requirements for Colonial Daughters of 17th Century (prior to 1700), and Colonial Dames of 17th Century (prior to 1701) are similar but with slightly different eligibility dates.

First settler societies define "service" as residing in a certain location prior to a specific date. One example of this is the Order of First Families of New Hampshire, which qualifies any ancestor who resided, owned land, or conducted business in New Hampshire before 1680. The Jamestowne Society honors ancestors who helped settle the colony of Jamestowne before 1700, including some investors in the Virginia Company who never set foot in Virginia.

Founder societies are similar to first settler societies but usually have a more limited listing of ancestors. The best-known example of a Founder Society is the General Society of Mayflower Descendants. Of the 102 Mayflower passengers who arrived at Plymouth in 1620, only 26 families left descendants.

Service also can be defined by the occupation of an ancestor. The Guild of Colonial Artisans and Tradesmen honors ancestors with occupations such as blacksmiths, butchers, and millers. The Descendants of Textile Workers honors ancestors in the weaving and clothing industry. The Descendants of Fossors recognizes ancestors who worked as undertakers and gravediggers.

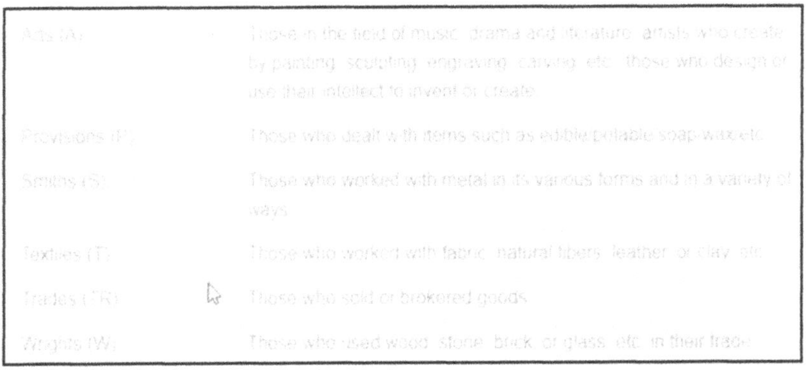

Arts (A)	Those in the field of music, drama and literature; artists who create by painting, sculpting, engraving, carving, etc.; those who design or use their intellect to invent or create
Provisions (P)	Those who dealt with items such as edible/potable/soap/wax/etc.
Smiths (S)	Those who worked with metal in its various forms and in a variety of ways
Textiles (T)	Those who worked with fabric, natural fibers, leather, or clay, etc.
Trades (TR)	Those who sold or brokered goods
Wrights (W)	Those who used wood, stone, brick, or glass, etc. in their trade

Figure 4.3 – The Guild of Colonial Artisans and Tradesmen considers six categories (or minor guilds) of ancestors for membership.

Service may also be defined by the religion of an ancestor. Some examples are the Descendants of Early Quakers and the National Huguenot Society.

The other thing to consider regarding eligibility is lineage. Almost all societies require documentation of direct lineage from the applicant to the ancestor. This documentation will be discussed in more detail in Chapter 6. You must be able to prove all generational linkages from yourself to your ancestor. A few societies will accept collateral ancestors. One example is the Descendants of American Prisoners of War, in which descent from a sibling of the qualifying ancestor is allowed.

Finally, it is important to know whether you qualify based on your age and gender. Most societies accept adults over 18 years old. Some accept younger members, such as the Associated Daughters of Early American Witches which accepts women over 16, or the Women Descendants of the Ancient and Honorable Artillery Company, which accepts women over 18 and also boys and girls under 18. Some societies specific for children under 21 include the Children of American Colonists and Children of the American Revolution.

Many Societies are open to both male and female members, but some are limited to one sex or the other, such as those bearing the designations "Daughters" or "Dames" and "Sons."

CHAPTER 5

BEGINNING THE APPLICATION PROCESS

The first step in joining a specific society is to learn about them. Peruse their website or Facebook page so you will have an idea of how active they are, if their meetings are convenient to attend, what their mission is, and of course, if you are eligible.

Once you have determined that you would indeed like to join a certain society, you will need to contact them and receive an application. A few societies have applications online, but most are obtained from the society's registrar.

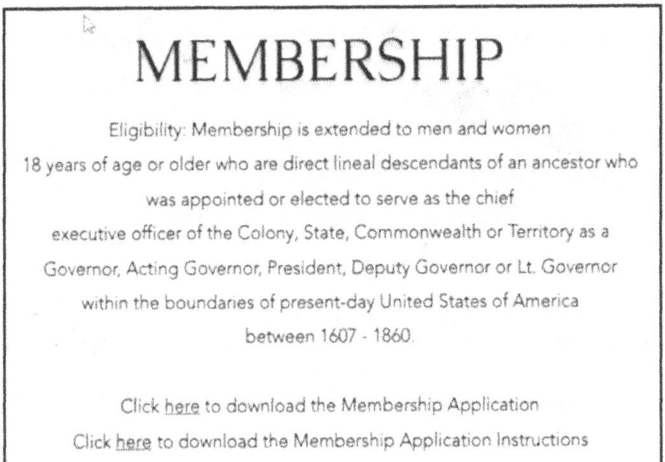

MEMBERSHIP

Eligibility: Membership is extended to men and women
18 years of age or older who are direct lineal descendants of an ancestor who
was appointed or elected to serve as the chief
executive officer of the Colony, State, Commonwealth or Territory as a
Governor, Acting Governor, President, Deputy Governor or Lt. Governor
within the boundaries of present-day United States of America
between 1607 - 1860.

Click here to download the Membership Application
Click here to download the Membership Application Instructions

Figure 5.1 – earlygovernors.org eligibility criteria with a downloadable application.

A few societies are strictly invitation only and frown on being contacted directly by an applicant. These societies rely on member referrals for new members. Because of this, they are not discussed further in this book.

Some societies might have a policy of "Invitation Only, Inquiries Welcome." It is acceptable to contact them. Often it is the Society President who is listed as the point of contact. They will then issue the invitation and instruct the Registrar to send an application. This is a way for the society to know who is interested and in the process of applying.

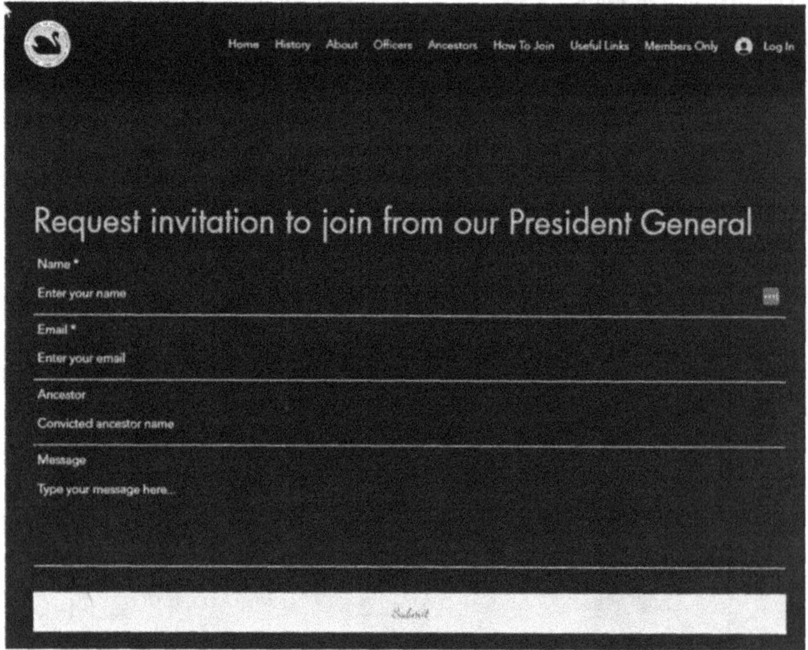

Figure 5.2 – The Associated Daughters of Early American Witches has an interest form on their website.

The majority of societies are open to anyone who wishes to apply. If the society has state or local chapters, their website usually contains a listing with either a link to the local website or an email address. It is best to contact the local chapter directly. If the society has only a national presence, the registrar usually has an email address on the website.

To digress a moment, different societies have different titles for their officers. The presiding officer may be called the President General, National President, or Governor General. The Registrar is the officer who assists with and approves the lineage in the application. Some societies call this person the Genealogist. In the Society of Mayflower Descendants, this person is the Historian. One of my favorite terms for this position is Keeper of Epitaphs in the Descendants of Fossors (whose term for the Presiding Officer is Chief Coroner). To keep it simple, this position will be referred to as Registrar in the sections that follow.

Once you are in touch with the Registrar, they will send you the application form as well as instructions on how to fill it out. In the larger societies with multiple chapters, the local registrar will assist the applicant in proving their lineage and completing the application. Application forms vary by society, so it is important to read the directions on how to complete them.

Several societies have published lineage books containing summaries of the lineages of their members. These may be helpful when compiling an application, but their admissibility as evidence varies with the society, as older lineages were not necessarily documented by today's standards.

The Registrar should provide directions on how to complete the application. This includes such things as the size of paper (letter vs legal), type of paper (some specify 25% cotton archival quality), print single or double-sided, number of copies to submit, and so on. They will advise where to send the completed copy, how much the application fee will be, as well as to whom to make out the check.

The documentation required for the lineage portion of the application will be discussed in Chapter 6. Proving the service of the ancestor is discussed in Chapter 7.

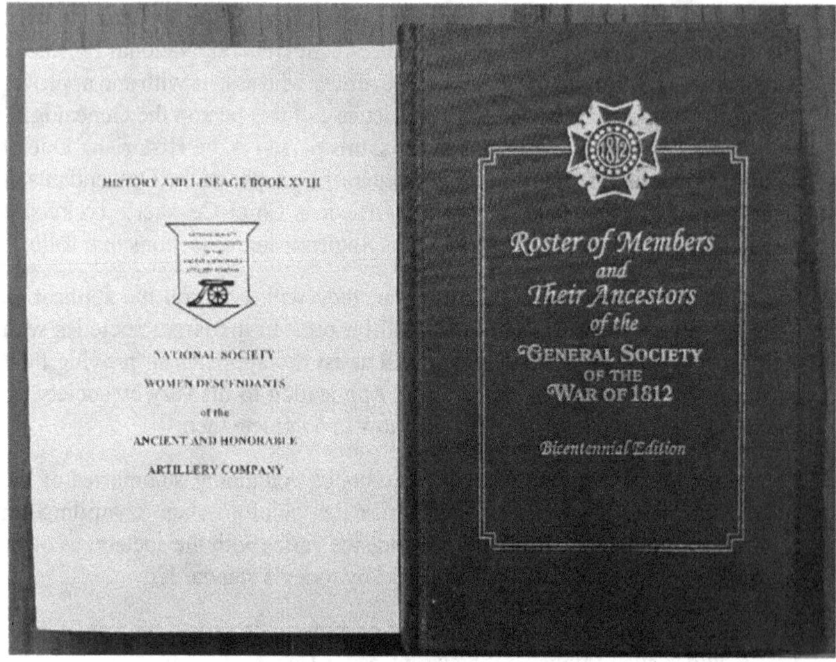

Figure 5.3 – Examples of published lineage books.

CHAPTER 6

DOCUMENTING YOUR LINEAGE

This is the most important portion of the application and will be the most time-consuming. Because these societies are based on lineal descent, the proof of lineage must be shown. This is done according to basic genealogical principles to show important dates and relationships of the people listed on the form.

Most applications have blanks for birth date and location, death date and location, and marriage date and location for each couple from the applicant to the proposed ancestor. Each of those blanks should be completed, if possible; again, this requirement varies a little with each society.

Common sources used to document your lineage are listed below. Many can be obtained online through sites like FamilySearch, Ancestry, American Ancestors, and so on. Some of the online sites are subscription-based, such as Ancestry, but many community libraries have free access for their patrons.

It has been estimated that less than 10 percent of genealogical records are online; therefore, some sources may require contacting the courthouse or archive where the event took place. Luckily, the most common record categories used for applications are online.

Many of the online sites have family trees that have been submitted by their users. These sites are <u>not</u> to be used as a source of documentation because many have errors. They may be useful for clues, however.

While a published transcription or record abstract may be obtained in a library, it is best to have a copy of the original record if possible. Similarly, there may be only an index record available online making it necessary to obtain a copy of the actual record or certificate.

The Registrar of the society may be able to help you determine if your line has been documented previously. This can help reduce the documentation needed for the generations you have in common with the previous applicant.

Vital Records

These are some of the first documents that a genealogist might collect and include birth, marriage, and death records. Occasionally divorce records are included in this category. Vital records usually are issued by the county or state in question. Birth and death records exist for most states since the late 19th or early 20th century. New England vital records were kept at the town level from the 1600's.

No. 22

Illinois State Board of Health.

Return of a Marriage to County Clerk.

1. Full Name of Groom: Basil Ormsby
2. Place of Residence: [illegible] Cumberland Co. Ill
3. Occupation: farming
4. Age Next Birthday: 22 Years. Color: W Race
5. Place of Birth: Cumberland Co. Ill
6. Father's Name: E. G. Ormsby
7. Mother's Maiden Name: Ela [illegible]
8. Number of Groom's Marriage: 1st
9. Full Name of Bride: Jessie Hill

   Maiden Name if a Widow
10. Place of Residence: Casey, Ill.
11. Age Next Birthday: 22 Years. Color: W Race
12. Place of Birth: Casey, Ill.
13. Father's Name: C. P. Hill
14. Mother's Maiden Name: Lone Wiley
15. Number of Bride's Marriage: 1st
16. Married at Effingham, Ill. in the County of Effingham and State of Illinois the 6th day of January 1917
17. Witnesses to Marriage: Ida Mappora, Eva Mapora

January 6th 1917

We hereby certify that the information above given is correct, to the best of our knowledge and belief.

Basil Ormsby (Groom)

Jessie Hill (Bride)

I hereby certify that the above is a correct return of a marriage solemnized by me.

Barney Overbeck

County Judge

Dated at Effingham this 6th day of January 1917

Figure 6.1 – Some marriage records can be a wealth of information, with age, birthplace, and parents' names.

Marriage records usually date to the formation of the county. Early records simply listed the names of the bride and groom, along with the date and location of their marriage. Later records include more information about the two parties, including information about their ages, birthplaces, and parents' names.

County boundaries changed frequently during the early years of our country. An ancestor may have lived in two or three counties without ever having moved, simply because the county boundary changed. The county-level records will be located in the county that was in existence at the time of the event. Two good references for these county boundary changes are the Newberry Library's Atlas of Historical County Boundaries at digital.newberry.org/ahcb, and the *Map Guide to the U.S. Federal Censuses, 1790-1920*[1].

Indices of vital records are available at several online sites; however, it is best to obtain the original record when possible. Not only is it less likely to have transcription errors, but there may be more information on the original record. The record does not need to be certified, and only a photocopy of the record should be submitted with the application as documentation is usually not returned to the applicant.

---

[1] Thorndale, William and Dollarhide, William, *Map Guide to the U.S. Federal Censuses, 1790-1920,* Baltimore: Genealogical Publishing Company, 1987.

Last Name	First Name	Middle Name	Sex/Race	Age	Cert No.	Death Date	County	City	Date Filed
HILL	CHARLEY	TAYLOR	M/W	UNK	0120033	1923-02-17	CLARK	CASEY	23-02-20

STATE OF ILLINOIS - STATE DEPARTMENT OF PUBLIC HEALTH - DIVISION OF VITAL STATISTICS
CERTIFICATE OF DEATH

137

County of Clark

Figure 6.2 – The index listing for a death certificate (ilsos.gov) is shown above the actual certificate. Note how much more information can be found in the actual record.

Substitutes for Vital Records

Before the government began keeping vital records, there are a few other sources to search for birth, marriage, and death information. Church records are helpful in this regard, as they may include marriage information, Baptism information and date of burial services, all of which can substitute for governmental records.

Family Bible records are also very useful and often predate civil vital records. These can be found in various locations – some are published, and other copies may be located at local historical or genealogical societies, or in local libraries.

Those who were born before their county began keeping birth records but lived into the mid-twentieth century may have a Delayed Birth Record. These were often obtained for World War II military service or applying for a Social Security number. They can be located at the county of birth but may be in a separate volume.

Cemetery Records

Photographs of tombstones may help prove the birth and death dates of individuals. Sometimes the birth date must be calculated as only an age at death is given. Occasionally there may be other information such as a marriage date, or a definite indication of a relationship (i.e.. "wife of..." or "child of...."). Online tombstone sites such as FindaGrave.com or Billiongraves.com are useful for locating photographs of tombstones. Any other user-submitted information on those sites, however, is considered as unreliable as an online family tree.

The cemetery itself may have records of the burial, as well as information about other family members. It may be helpful to contact the cemetery, especially if it is currently in operation.

Census Records

The United States has conducted a census every 10 years since 1790. Except for the 1890 census, which was almost completely lost in a fire, they are available online through 1950. Beginning in 1850, the census would list the name of every person in the household with an age and a birthplace (usually a state or foreign country). This information can be helpful for the birth information on the application. Beginning in 1880, the relationship to the head of household was also listed, although familial assumptions may be acceptable based on the 1850, 1860, and 1870 censuses. Caution must be used, however, when assuming that the apparent wife is truly the mother of the listed children, and societies may require additional documentation of that relationship.

Later censuses include information on how long the couple had been married, how many children they had, and even the months of birth of the listed individuals.

The mortality schedules from 1850-1880 may help narrow down a death date. These schedules list those individuals who died in the 12 months preceding that census; for example, the 1850 mortality schedule lists those who died between 1 June 1849 and 31 May 1850. These are especially helpful because many jurisdictions did not keep death records that early.

Several states also conducted state censuses at intervals between the federal censuses. These may contain additional information on vital statistics or familial relationships.

SCHEDULE 3.—Persons who Died during the Year ending 1st June, 1860, in ... in the County of Sauk State of Wisconsin, enumerated by me, ...

Figure 6.3 – The 1860 mortality schedule for Sauk County, Wisconsin. The month of death and cause of death are also listed.

Newspapers

Newspapers are wonderful sources of information. The most obvious source is the obituary of an individual which may give many other details about their life, parents, and spouse. Keep in mind that an obituary may be published in a location other than where the person died if they were a prominent person or long-time resident. Other helpful information in newspapers are announcements of engagements and marriages, as well as birth announcements.

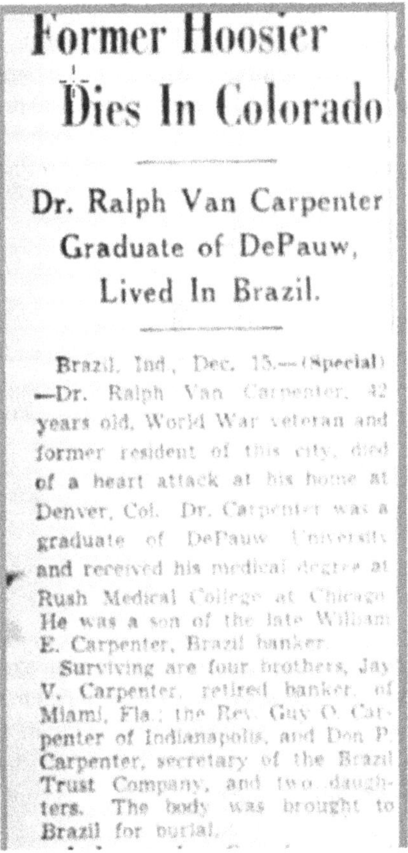

Former Hoosier Dies In Colorado

Dr. Ralph Van Carpenter Graduate of DePauw, Lived In Brazil.

Brazil, Ind., Dec. 15.—(Special) —Dr. Ralph Van Carpenter, 42 years old, World War veteran and former resident of this city, died of a heart attack at his home at Denver, Col. Dr. Carpenter was a graduate of DePauw University and received his medical degree at Rush Medical College at Chicago. He was a son of the late William E. Carpenter, Brazil banker.

Surviving are four brothers, Jay V. Carpenter, retired banker, of Miami, Fla.; the Rev. Guy O. Carpenter of Indianapolis, and Don P. Carpenter, secretary of the Brazil Trust Company, and two daughters. The body was brought to Brazil for burial.

Figure 6.4 – This Indiana newspaper obituary tells of a Colorado resident. His age, military service, and education are listed, in addition to his father, brothers, and daughters. (*Indianapolis Star,* 16 December 1940).

Local Histories

Many counties have published a local history, often to celebrate an anniversary year. These local histories were especially popular during the last quarter of the 19th century. Many are available online at sites such as Internet Archive (archive.org), Google Books (books.google.com), or Hathi Trust (hathitrust.org). These local histories often included biographies of the citizens of that county. They may be used as reference material provided that the book was published during the lifetime of the person being referenced, or shortly thereafter. Local histories also can provide clues for further research.

Family Histories

It may be tempting to use a published family history for an application. Caution is recommended, as many early family histories did not cite their sources and, therefore are not acceptable. Those published more recently tend to have better documentation. They can be useful as clues to help find the records.

Probate Records

Probate records may be very helpful, especially for the generations prior to birth records. They may be obtained from the county court where the individual resided at their death, or another county where they owned property at their death. More and more of these records are becoming available online. If the individual wrote a will, it is possible that they specified their children by name, including the married names of any daughters. Intestate papers and contested wills provide useful information as well, as heirs were usually listed. It may be necessary to request the full probate packet from the county courthouse and not rely simply on the copy in the will book.

Land Records

Land records and deeds also may be used to help document relationships. They are available from the county court where the land was owned. It is important to realize that county boundaries may have shifted over time so the land records may be located in the county where the land was at the time of the deed, not in the present county. These records may note fathers selling land to their children. It is wonderful if the child is so noted but selling land for nominal sums (like one dollar) or "for love and affection" is a helpful clue. It may be possible that the land simply passed down from generation to generation and the deed was not recorded until years later, so it is important to expand your search past the death date of the individual being researched.

Figure 6.5 – Land records at a county courthouse.

Pension Records

Military Pension records can be helpful. They can be obtained from the National Archives in Washington, D.C.; those from earlier wars are being digitized and placed online at Fold3.com. Pensions received by widows of veterans are especially useful because the widow had to prove their marriage, as well as the veteran's death.

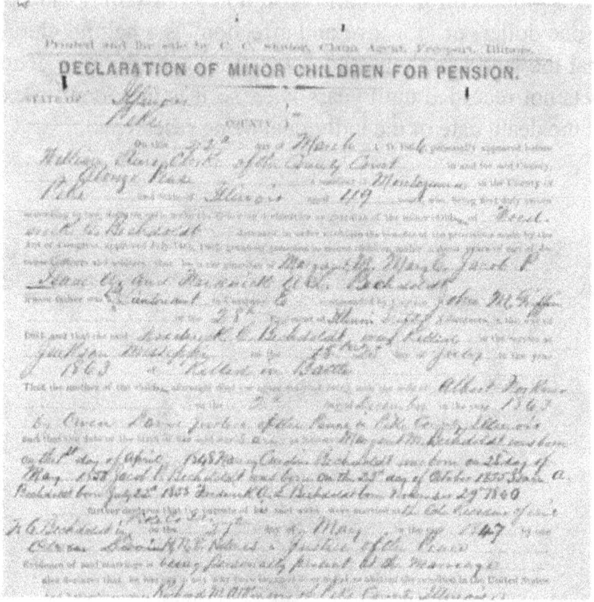

DECLARATION OF MINOR CHILDREN FOR PENSION.

Figure 6.6 – A page from a pension application from a surviving minor child. Information includes military service, marriage information, other children, and much more.

Other Records

Published genealogies may be acceptable if they include source citations for each fact. Unfortunately, many early family histories were not documented; however, they may be used for clues to locate acceptable documentation. Articles in reputable genealogical journals, such as the *National Genealogical Society Quarterly, New England Historical Genealogical Register,* and *The American Genealogist* usually are acceptable.

There are several other sources that genealogists may use to determine relationships. These include other court records, and other newspaper records, for example, that can be help build an argument for the parental connection.

Some of this documentation may require using indirect evidence to show relationships. A simple example involves two documents: one that states Person B was the child of Person A, and another that states Person C was the sibling of Person B; therefore proving that Person C was also the child of Person A.

Previous Applications

It is tempting to use a society's published lineage book as documentation. Unfortunately, many of these lineages may no longer be acceptable under current standards of genealogy. They may require additional documentation that might not have been available at the time of the previous application. Thus, these books are useful only for clues to the lineage.

Similarly, an applicant who is joining a society on the same line that their grandparent used may be required to update the documentation. However, the earlier application can provide clues to the lineage.

Some societies will honor a copy of an approved application from another society as "documentation". These policies are society specific and vary regarding what is or is not acceptable.

It is understood that not all dates and locations will be found, especially for the earlier generations. However, most societies will insist on full details for the most recent three generations or so.

In all cases, it is important to remember that the link between generations must be shown. It is not enough to include dates and places of vital events; rather, the actual descent from the ancestor must be proven.

Table 1 - Vital information that may be found in various records.

Type of Record	**Birth**	**Marriage**	**Death**	**Parentag**
Birth record	X			X
Birth certificate	X			X
Marriage license application	X	X		X
Marriage record		X		
Death record	X		X	X
Death certificate	X		X	X
Baptism record	X			X
Bible record	X	X	X	X
Burial record	X		X	X
Birth announcement	X			X
Mariage announcement		X		X
Obituary	X	X	X	X
Census	Age	Some		Some
Mortality schedule	Age		X	
Cemetery records/tombstones	X		X	
Probate records			X	X
Land records			X	X
Military records	X	Some	X	
Pension records	X	Some	X	
Local Histories	X	X	X	X

CHAPTER 7

DOCUMENTING YOUR ANCESTOR'S QUALIFYING SERVICE

The qualifying "service" of the ancestor can range from military or civil service, to having a particular occupation or religion, to simply being an early settler, depending on the specific society. The details of what constitutes service should be found on the individual society's website or in the application instructions.

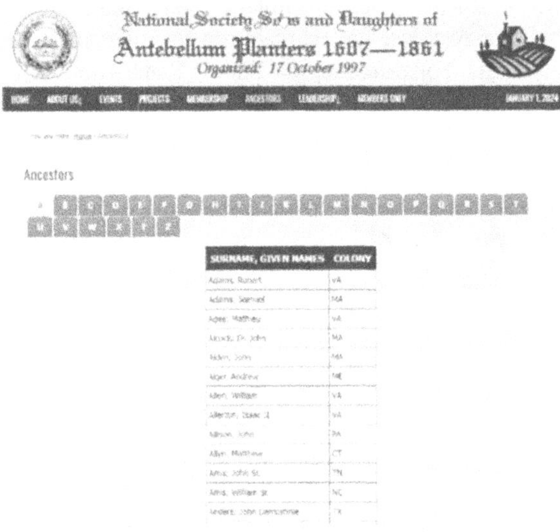

Figure 7.1 – Proven ancestors listed on antebellumplanters.org.

Often, the society has a listing of ancestors who qualify, although proof must be provided that your specific ancestor is the same one on that list. Some society listings may be complete, such as those of the Society of Mayflower Descendants, or the Women Descendants of the Ancient and Honorable Artillery Company; all qualifying ancestors for these societies are known.

Other listings may be non-exhaustive, meaning that additional qualified ancestors may be proven. These lists of ancestors may be published on the society's website.

Sources for Military Service

Societies that honor service in a particular war or wars often will require proof of military service. There are several possible sources for locating this service, such as a muster roll, a pension record for that ancestor, or similar documentation.

Colonial and antebellum conflicts often have published muster rolls. These may be located in a genealogical or military library, and some are online. The National and State Archives also contain muster rolls and rosters of various military companies. For example, the Illinois State Archives contains many such documents related to the Illinois units that fought in the Civil War.

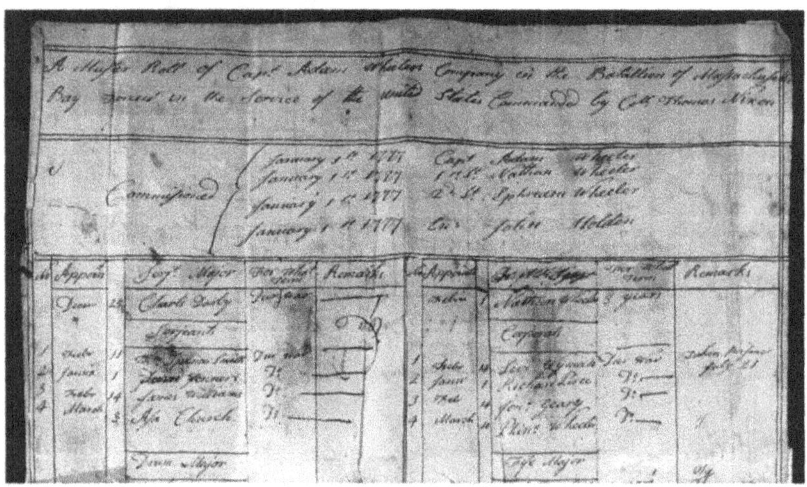

Figure 7.2 – a muster roll for a Massachusetts militia in the Revolutionary War (familysearch.org).

Pension records of our ancestors or their widows are very helpful for documenting their military service. The veteran had to provide proof that he served during a particular time, in a particular unit, and for specific dates in order to receive the pension. These records are often a good source of genealogical information as well.

Prior to the Civil War, the veteran might be paid in Bounty Land instead of cash, as the Federal government was cash-poor but land-rich. Applications for Bounty Land also contain information about the veteran's service.

Pension records and Bounty Land applications can be found at the National Archives. They are slowly being digitized and made available on Fold3.com. Some states issued their own pensions or bounty lands, and those records are usually located in the State Archives.

Some societies will require specific military service. For example, the Dames of the Loyal Legion requires the ancestor to have served as an officer in the Civil War, in contrast to enlisted service. The Dames of the Court of Honor similarly requires that the ancestor served as an officer in any colonial or United States war prior to and including the Civil War.

The Women Descendants of the Ancient and Honorable Artillery Company recognizes ancestors who were members of that company in Boston prior to the American Revolution. There is a published listing of all qualifying ancestors available. [2] Some of these Society's published listings may include genealogical information for a few generations.

Other military service during the colonial period might be found in court records where the ancestor lived. He may have received payment from the town for his service.

---

[2] Kallal, Jeannine Sheldon. *Genealogical Data of the Ancient & Honorable Artillery Company of Massachusetts, 1638-1774.* Revised edition. n.p.: National Society Women Descendants of the Ancient & Honorable Artillery Company of Massachusetts, 2020.

Civil or Patriotic Service

Both the Daughters of the American Revolution and the Sons of the American Revolution include ancestors who provided civil or patriotic service as well as military service during the Revolutionary War.

Serving as an elected official is an example of civil service. Patriotic service can be anything that supports the cause. An ancestor may have donated food for the troops or paid a supply tax. Records of patriotic service may often be found in court documents, receipts, or tax lists. Some of these records have been published or made available online. The Daughters of the American Revolution has published a series of Source Guides for the colonies that identify several locations where these records may be found.[3]

It is important to review the criteria for the society you wish to join. For example, the Sons of the Revolution (SR, as opposed to SAR), honors only military service during the Revolutionary War. Similarly, the General Society of 1812 accepts only military service during a four-year period (1811-1815), while the Daughters of 1812 accepts military or civil service from the close of the American Revolution to the end of the War of 1812 (1784-1815).

The Continental Society Daughters of Indian Wars honors military service during several conflicts with Native Americans, but also recognizes ancestors who served in peaceful capacities such as traders and interpreters.

---

[3] One example is Grundset, Eric G. *Connecticut in the American Revolution: A Source Guide for Genealogists and Historians.* Washington: National Society Daughters of the American Revolution, 2016.

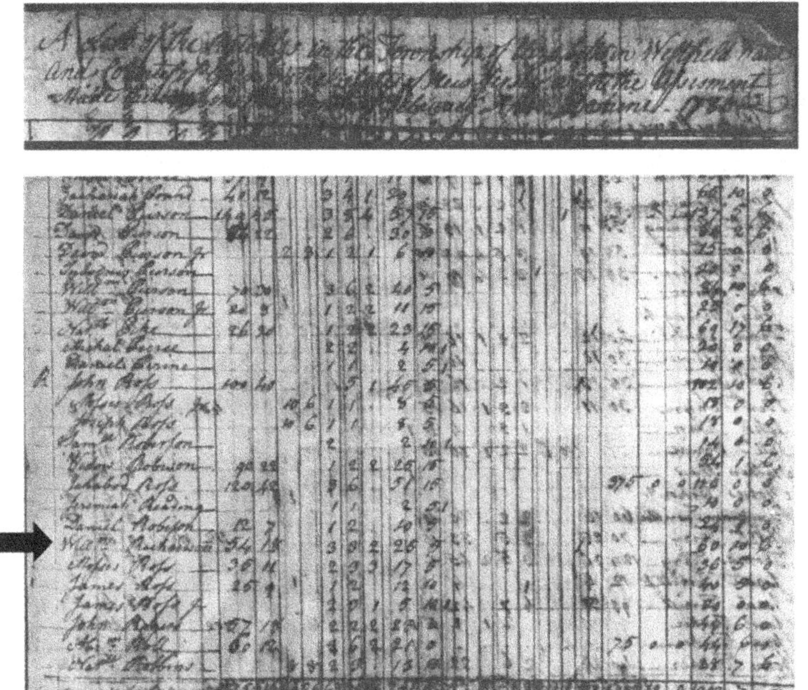

Figure 7.3 – Although difficult to read, this is an excerpt from a supply tax listing for Essex County, NJ. This tax was used to support the Revolutionary Army and is one location where female patriots may be found (e.g. "Widow Robinson").

Sources for Civil Service

Civil Service can take many forms, and therefore can be found in many locations. Civil Service usually refers to some sort of official work. An ancestor may have been a prominent elected official, or simply a local citizen doing their duty. If a society accepts civil service as a qualifying service, they will define the extent of that service.

The more prominent the service, the easier it is to document. Elected officials may be listed in the history of the town or county. Government documents also may be useful, as they contain lists of representatives to their legislatures, or even names of those individuals in their minutes. Published histories are available at local libraries and online. The documents may have been transcribed or abstracted and may also be available at the state library. The original documents are usually held at the appropriate government archive (National or State).

Figure 7.4 – Court records like this may require time and patience to research.

Less prominent service can include appointed service such as a highway surveyor or a fence viewer. These activities would have been conducted by a local resident, and the duties usually passed from one person to the next every year or so. Service as a juror also may constitute civil service for certain societies. These appointments are usually included in the records of the individual town or county. Again, published local histories can be a good resource for these types of service.

Sources for First Settlers

Many societies honor ancestors who were the first in a specific area. The best-known example is the General Society of Mayflower Descendants. This society honors only those 102 ancestors who traveled on the *Mayflower* to settle in Plymouth colony in 1620. These ancestors have been extensively researched and publications listing the first several generations of their descendants are available in several genealogical libraries.[4]

Some of these societies have published lists of the known first settlers. The Descendants of the Founders of Ancient Windsor accepts descent only from the first settlers of that town. A listing of qualifying ancestors is included on their website.

Other first settler societies include ancestors who can be proven to be in a certain location before a certain date. The majority of First Family societies are like this. An example is the Descendants of Cape Cod and the Islands, whose qualifying ancestors were residents, landowners, or businessmen in that region prior to 1700. The list is incomplete and "new" ancestors may be added if they can be shown to qualify. Histories of the region are the best starting point for documentation of this type of service.

The Sons and Daughters of the Pilgrims does not limit itself to the traditional *Mayflower* "Pilgrim" but extends to any ancestor who settled in the original colonies prior to 1700. Proof of residence can be found in several types of records, including vital records, land records, and so on. This type of society is continually accepting new ancestors as they are proven.

Qualifying ancestors for "first settler" societies of a later era may be proven with census records and tax lists that show an ancestor in a certain location on a given date. Some examples of these are the First Families of Ohio, Prairie Pioneers (Illinois), and Daughters of Utah Pioneers.

---

[4] Mayflower Society. *Mayflower Families Through Five Generations.* (several volumes).

Sources for Occupations

This type of documentation may be a little harder to track down but can be found in town records, court records, or probate records. For example, the Guild of Colonial Artisans and Tradesmen honors ancestors who practiced one of several types of trades. A local history may describe an ancestor as running a mill, which would qualify him as a millwright. Probate records, especially inventories, may include a reference to a particular occupation; for example, if blacksmith tools are inventoried, the deceased was likely a blacksmith.

If the qualifying period extends into the 19th century, census records may also be helpful. An example is a notation in the census that the ancestor was a Postmaster. That would qualify as service for the Descendants of Early Postmasters. Other more modern sources may include city directories or newspapers. Obituaries and death certificates may indicate the occupation of the deceased.

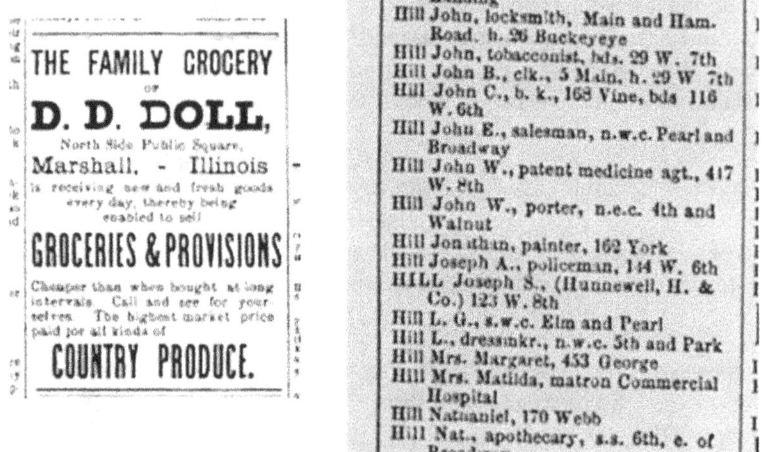

Landing
Hill John, locksmith, Main and Ham. Road, h. 26 Buckeyeye
Hill John, tobacconist, bds. 29 W. 7th
Hill John B., clk., 5 Main, h. 29 W 7th
Hill John C., b. k., 168 Vine, bds 116 W. 6th
Hill John E., salesman, n.w.c. Pearl and Broadway
Hill John W., patent medicine agt., 417 W. 8th
Hill John W., porter, n.e.c. 4th and Walnut
Hill Jonathan, painter, 162 York
Hill Joseph A., policeman, 144 W. 6th
HILL Joseph S., (Hunnewell, H. & Co.) 123 W. 8th
Hill L. G., s.w.c. Elm and Pearl
Hill L., dressmkr., n.w.c. 5th and Park
Hill Mrs. Margaret, 453 George
Hill Mrs. Matilda, matron Commercial Hospital
Hill Nathaniel, 170 Webb
Hill Nat., apothecary, s.s. 6th, e. of

Figure 7.5 – This newspaper ad (*Marshall Herald*, 3 February 1897) can be used to prove D.D. Doll was a grocer, while this 1860 Cincinnati City Directory lists several occupations.

An oft-heard lament from prospective members is "All I have are farmers." The National Society Descendants of American Farmers honors the ordinary ancestor. Documentation of farming can be found in census records, probate records, and local histories.

Sources for Religions

Some societies require ancestors to be of a certain religion. The Descendants of Early Quakers is an example. Luckily, the Quakers themselves kept very good records of their meetings, many of which have been published. Finding mention of an ancestor who took part in a meeting, or whose vital records are included in the meeting records, provides documentation of that religion.

Figure 7.6 – earlyquakers.org has several suggestions for locating Quaker records.

Other religions may not be as easy to prove. The National Huguenot Society has published listings of known Huguenot ancestors (French Protestants who escaped religious persecution).[5] They also are compiling some other finding aids, such as a listing of Revolutionary patriots with Huguenot connections. Morton and Henderson's book on church records may be helpful in locating records from certain religions.[6]

Service as a broad category

Many societies consider "service" as a very broad category. Two examples are the Colonial Daughters of the Seventeenth Century and the Daughters of the American Colonists. Essentially, any ancestor who did anything noteworthy during the society's time frame may be acceptable, including military service, civil service, and original land ownership. The preceding suggestions for locating documentation will apply. The best approach is to work with the society's Registrar if you are unsure if a particular documentation of service is acceptable.

Other types of service

The Associated Daughters of Early American Witches has qualifying "service" that doesn't really fit into the above categories. To join, members must prove descent from someone who was accused, tried, or convicted of witchcraft before 1700. That society has published a listing of qualifying ancestors that contains brief genealogical information as well.[7]

---

[5] Kallal, Jeannine Sheldon. *Register of Qualified Huguenot Ancestors of the National Huguenot Society*. Fifth edition. San Antonio: National Huguenot Society, 2012.

[6] Morton, Sunny Jane and Henderson, Harold A. *How to Find Your Family History in U.S. Church Records: A Genealogist's Guide.* Baltimore: Genealogical Publishing company, 2019.

[7] Nagy, Kimberly Ormsby. *Associated Daughters of Early American Witches Roll of Ancestors.* Second edition. Berwyn Heights, MD: Heritage Books, 2022.

CHAPTER 8

COMPLETING THE APPLICATION

Once you have gathered the necessary documentation proving your lineage to your ancestor, and the documentation for their qualifying service, it is time to complete the application. Each society has its own format of application to complete, but they are similar in the type of information requested. All have spaces to record the dates and locations of births, marriages, and deaths for the lineage. All have a place to list the source documentation for each generation. Every application has a location to list the ancestor's service and documentation.

It is important to read the instructions for the application that are provided by the society. Local and state registrars can be very helpful in filling out applications.

Information about the applicant and their ancestor

The first page of most applications usually consists of information about the applicant: their full name, address, phone number, and email. There may be a place to list how they want their name to appear on the certificate. The ancestor's name is often included on the first page, along with a place to list their qualifying service. Occasionally, more information about the qualifying ancestor is requested; for example, their birth and death year, or the location of their service. The first page normally is where the applicant signs attesting to the lineage to the best of their knowledge. If the applicant is applying to a society that has state or local chapters, there usually is a place for the local registrar to sign stating that they agree with the lineage. Often, the local presiding officer, or perhaps other members, will sign to signify that the applicant is welcome in their chapter assuming the lineage is correct. Finally, there is a place for the national registrar to sign signifying that the lineage has been verified, and the member's national number and date of acceptance are added.

Descendants of Fossors 1607-1860

Application for Membership

Founded in 2014

Name:

I wish my name to appear on my certificate as:

Address:

City: State: ZIP-4:

Telephone: E-mail:

I hereby apply for membership in the **DESCENDANTS OF FOSSORS** by virtue of direct descent from:

of the state colony of ,

who was born in the year and died in the year ,

and served as (gravedigger, *inquisito post mortem*, sexton, &c.), as proved by the following documentation:

This application is correct to the best my knowledge and belief.

Signature of Applicant — Date

DO NOT WRITE BELOW THIS LINE

Genealogy approved by ______________________________

Date approved ______________ **Fee paid $**_______ **Check #** _______

Membership Number

Figure 8.1 – A typical first page of an application with applicant's contact information, ancestor's service, and lines for signatures.

Occasionally, the service of the ancestor may be listed on the last page of the application. If so, usually more information is requested, such as the location where they served, the date of their service, and details about their military service or occupation, depending on the society. Again, the documentation of the service will be included near the above information. Some societies ask for more information about the ancestor's family such as a listing of their children, or information about additional spouses. This is usually to help subsequent applicants by providing additional clues to the ancestor's family.

ANCESTOR'S SERVICE

The said ______ who resided during the American Revolution at ______

assisted in establishing American independence while acting in the capacity of ______

for the state/country of ______, Ancestor Number ______

A description of my ancestor's services during the Revolutionary War were as follows: (THIS FIELD CANNOT BE LEFT BLANK)

Give source citations of acceptable proof for Military, Civil or Patriotic Service. When proving new service, or updating current service, a copy of the proof **must** be submitted. (THIS FIELD CANNOT BE LEFT BLANK)

Application Verified ______ Accepted by the National Board ______

Registrar General ______

Recording Secretary General ______

The names of spouses and children listed below do not constitute proof of lineal descent from the Revolutionary patriot except for the spouse and child listed in the lineage on page two of this application.

My Revolutionary ancestor was married *(This section is OPTIONAL)*

(1) to ______ at ______ in ______

(2) to ______ at ______ in ______

(3) to ______ at ______ in ______

(4) to ______ at ______ in ______

CHILDREN OF REVOLUTIONARY ANCESTOR *(This section is OPTIONAL)*

As proven by:

NAMES	DATES OF BIRTH – PLACE	TO WHOM MARRIED, NOTE IF MORE THAN ONE

Figure 8.2 – The last page of the Daughters of the American Revolution application with a detailed section for the ancestor's service, along with information about their children.

Listing the lineage

The lineage of the applicant usually begins on the second page. The most common type of application begins with the applicant as Generation #1, their parents as Generation #2, and so on, back to the qualifying ancestor. Other than generation #1 (the applicant), the male is listed first in each generation, regardless of which parent the lineage goes through. There is a section to fill out for each generation that includes dates and locations of vital events.

1. I was born on ______ at ______
married on ______ at ______
to ______ born on ______ at ______
living ☐ or died on ______ at ______
Proof ______

2. I am the (son/daughter) of
______ born on ______ at ______
died on ______ at ______
married on ______ at ______ to
wife ______ born on ______ at ______
died on ______ at ______
Proof ______

3. The said ______ was the (son/daughter) of
______ born on ______ at ______

Figure 8.3 – A typical lineage section of an application with spaces for birth, marriage, and death dates and locations.

Some societies (i.e. Daughters of the American Revolution) require complete dates and locations for the first three generations, with earlier generations having at least one event listed. It is best to have as much information for each generation as possible. Often, earlier generations may not have exact dates or places, but estimates can be entered. If a birth date is unknown, but can be approximated to a year, this is shown by entering "circa [year]". If a death date is unknown, an approximation can be given, such as a date the will was probated "wp [date]," or even the last known date of record as in "liv [year]," If only a state of death is known, that is all that is entered. Death locations also may be approximated by the county of probate, or the location of the cemetery, as in "wp [county, state]" or "bur [county, state]."

A few societies list the generations in reverse order; in other words, starting with the ancestor as Generation #1, the ancestor's child and spouse as Generation #2, and so on, down to the applicant. These applications list the line-carrying child first in each generation, regardless of whether it is the husband or wife of the couple.

Statement of Line of Eligibility for membership in the Society of the Descendants of the Colonial Clergy.

EVERY NAME OF A PERSON MUST BE WRITTEN IN FULL. DO NOT USE INITIALS!

1. Rev._____ born at_____ on_____ son of _____, was graduated at _____ (College) _____ (Year) ordained at_____ on_____

settled at_____ (Church) _____ (Town) _____ (Colony) (-);
died at_____ on_____, married at_____
on_____ to_____ born at_____
on_____, died at_____ on_____. Their_____ (Son or Daughter) was
References:

2._____ born at_____ on_____
died at_____ on_____, married at_____
on_____, to_____ born at_____
on_____, died at_____ on_____. Their_____ (Son or Daughter) was
References:

Figure 8.4 – This application begins with the ancestor, then continues to their child, and so on. The applicant is listed last.

Listing the documentation

The documentation used for each generation may be listed following each generational section, or on a subsequent page. The Society of Mayflower Descendants has abbreviated documentation following each event. In fact, the Mayflower Society does not require documentation for the first few generations, because the early generations have been extensively documented, and every applicant uses that same documentation.

The majority of documentation will need to be listed. Every society has its own system as to how detailed the citation should be. A birth certificate may be listed as "BC" or "Birth cert". A census record may be simply "[year] U.S. census" or may be more detailed. A land record or will should have, at minimum, the type of record, the county and state, and the volume number and page of the original record. A published book may have a full citation, or simply the author's last name and a short title. While good genealogical practice is to have a full "Evidence Explained" citation,[8] there is often not enough room on the application form. The instructions for each society will provide guidance.

Occasionally it is possible to use a previously submitted application for a portion of the lineage. This can be done if applying to the same society on the same line as one's relative. It also can be done when submitting a supplemental application for another ancestor. Some societies will provide redacted copies of previously approved applications for a fee, which may be helpful for earlier generations. Local registrars can assist with determining whether these earlier applications will be helpful.

In this case, most societies will still request a listing of the documentation used for the original application, with a notation that another application is being used. Again, refer to the instructions for the particular society.

Occasionally, a society will request a separate sheet listing the citations for all documentation used, listed as Document #1, Document #2, and so on. In these instances, all that is listed on the application itself are the document numbers used for each generation.

---

[8] Mills, Elizabeth Shown. *Evidence Explained: Citing History Sources from Artifacts to Cyberspace.* Fourth edition. Baltimore: Genealogical Publishing Company, 2024.

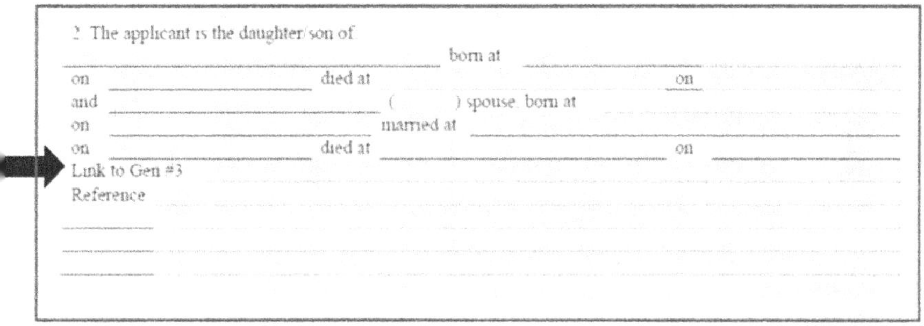

2 The applicant is the daughter/son of
born at
on died at on
and ( ) spouse born at
on married at
on died at on
Link to Gen #3
Reference

Figure 8.5 – This application emphasizes the importance of documenting the link between generations.

In all applications, the most important thing to prove is the connection between generations. A few applications even have a line to list the connecting document in addition to the documents for dates and places. For example, in figure 8.5, if a birth certificate is used to link generations 2 and 3, it would be listed on the indicated line.

Preparing the documentation

When preparing the documentation to submit, it is helpful to indicate the pertinent portions of the document. Always send a copy (not the original) of any certificates, as documentation is not usually returned. The pertinent information in the document is usually underlined with a red pen or pencil. It is very helpful to registrars if the family of interest has been underlined in a census or court record. Avoid using a highlighter as it will not copy well if the documentation is later digitized by the society. Be sure that the copy submitted is legible. It also may be helpful to enlarge a section of the census, to improve readability.

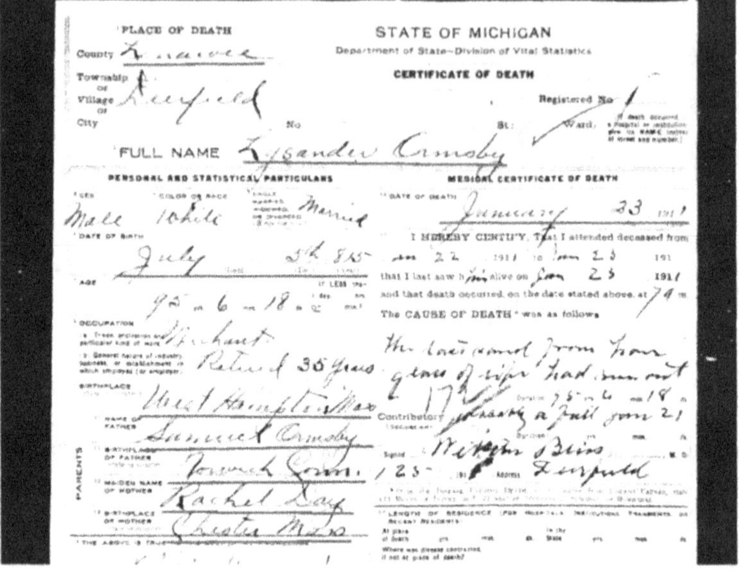
PLACE OF DEATH
STATE OF MICHIGAN
Department of State—Division of Vital Statistics
CERTIFICATE OF DEATH
County
Township or Village or City Deerfield
Registered No. 1
FULL NAME Lysander Ormsby
PERSONAL AND STATISTICAL PARTICULARS
MEDICAL CERTIFICATE OF DEATH
Sex: Male
Color or Race: White
Single, Married, Widowed or Divorced: Married
DATE OF DEATH January 23 1911
DATE OF BIRTH July 5th 1815
AGE 95 yrs 6 mo 18 d
I HEREBY CERTIFY, That I attended deceased from Jan 22 1911 to Jan 23 1911
that I last saw him alive on Jan 23 1911
and that death occurred, on the date stated above, at 7 a.m.
The CAUSE OF DEATH was as follows
OCCUPATION Merchant
Retired 35 years
BIRTHPLACE West Hampton Mass
NAME OF FATHER Samuel Ormsby
BIRTHPLACE OF FATHER Norwich Conn.
MAIDEN NAME OF MOTHER Rachel Day
BIRTHPLACE OF MOTHER Chester Mass
Address Deerfield
LENGTH OF RESIDENCE
Where was disease contracted, if not at place of death?

Figure 8.6 – All pertinent information has been underlined on this death certificate.

If a handwritten document such as a will or land record is submitted, include a transcription of, at minimum, the pertinent section.

If documentation is provided from a published book or a Bible, be sure to include the title page and the copyright page.

If an analysis is necessary to prove indirect evidence, that document should be appropriately labeled as such and be accompanied by copies of the information used in the analysis.

Each document should be labeled with the generations that it references. This may be done on the upper corner on the front of the document. Some societies request information on the back of the document such as the applicant's name, the chapter they are joining, and so on. This can be helpful if the documentation is separated from the application during processing.

Every date and place listed on the application should have accompanying documentation. One piece of documentation may support several facts, such as a Bible record with multiple generations. It is only necessary to send one copy of that document – don't overwhelm the Registrar with paper. Similarly, if a copy of an original record is provided, it is not necessary to include the index version of that record.

Be sure that all dates and locations make sense. The mother's birth date should be between (on average) sixteen and forty-five years before her child's birth date, and the father should not have died more than nine months before the child was born, and so on.

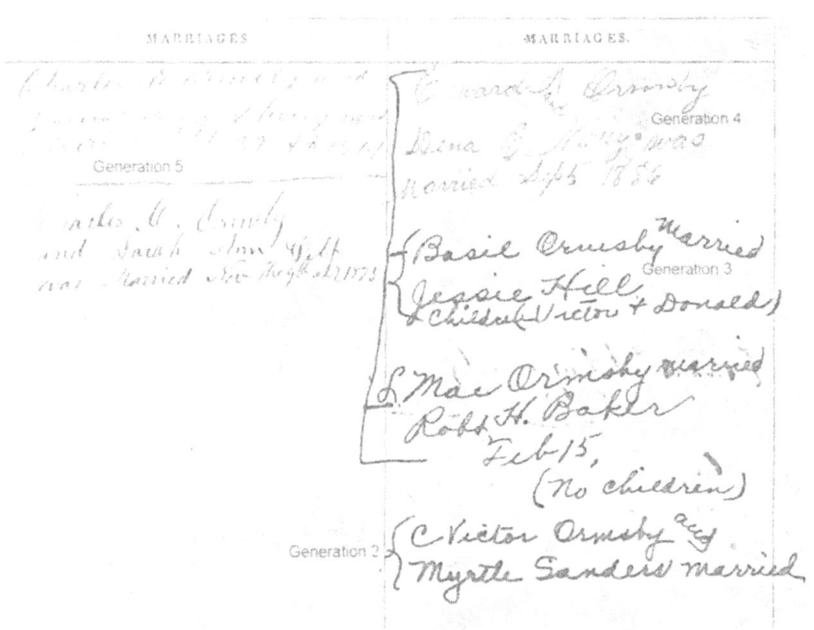

Figure 8.7 – This page from a family Bible has multiple generations noted. Only one copy of this document needs to be submitted.

Printing the application

Once the application has been completed, follow the directions of the society as to how it should be printed. Societies may request single- vs. double-sided applications, or letter vs. legal size paper. A few societies still require high quality archival paper, such as the type that is watermarked “25% cotton.”

Print out the required number of copies, sign each copy as the applicant, and be sure that any other necessary signatures are obtained. If additional signatures are needed, the local or state registrar will usually assist with that. Write a check for the required amount, again, determined by the individual society. Some societies request the first year of dues with the application, while others may have only a lifetime membership payable at the time of application.

The documentation should be placed in a logical order, i.e.. by generation. Paper clips are usually acceptable to keep generations together. Nothing should be stapled.

It is advisable to keep a copy of the application itself in case questions arise or another copy is needed.

CHAPTER 9

WHAT NEXT?

Waiting for Approval

Once you have submitted your application, you may be anxious to hear if you have been accepted. Acceptance times vary depending on the society. If you are applying to a smaller society that does not have local chapters, the application is usually sent directly to the verifying registrar. Approval times for these societies tend to be fairly brief. When I am the approving registrar for a society, I try to approve an application within a few days of receipt.

If the application requires additional signatures and/or approval from a chapter or state registrar, there is a natural delay while those signatures are being obtained. The larger societies tend to take longer for approval as well, simply because of the volume of applications that they receive.

Larger societies may also have additional stages between approval of the lineage (verification) and actual admission to membership. Admission to membership may be done only at certain times of the year, as when the National Board meets. The Daughters of the American Revolution admits new members on a monthly basis, while the Daughters of the American Colonists admits on a quarterly basis.

If a certificate is provided with the acceptance letter, there may be an additional delay in having the certificate printed or calligraphed.

On occasion, an application may not be approved on submission. The verifying registrar may ask for additional documentation for a generational link. If this happens, make an attempt to provide the necessary documentation. On a rare occasion, it may be necessary to substitute the lineage to that of another qualifying ancestor. In these circumstances, the verifying registrar is simply trying to have the best possible lineage, as these applications are a form of historic preservation.

Keep in mind that the majority of approving registrars are volunteers. In fact, all officers of these societies are volunteers. Only a few of the largest societies hire paid genealogists to verify applications.

After Approval

One day you will receive a letter that says "Congratulations! You are now a member of our society." This is cause to celebrate that your hard work documenting your lineage and your ancestor's service has paid off.

While some members are content with that knowledge, most lineage society members recognize that they receive the real benefits of joining these societies by becoming active.

Figure 9.1 – DAR and C.A.R., members in a local Independence Day parade.

Local chapter meetings are held throughout the year, usually at a location convenient to the members. These meetings usually have some brief business, followed by an interesting program. Many include time to meet and visit with other members, possibly during a meal. The members have at least one thing in common: similar ancestry. Most are at least hobby genealogists. In addition, the members usually have a similar interest in history, historic preservation, community service, or other focus of the society.

The smaller societies that do not have chapters will meet annually, many during a two week period in April in the Washington D.C. area known as "Lineage Fortnight". Other societies may meet at other times or locations during the year. The Descendants of Cape Cod and the Islands meets in the fall on Cape Cod Nantucket, or Martha's Vineyard. The Daughters of Indian Wars meets in the fall at a different location every year. Meetings of this sort usually include tours of local historic sites. In addition to an annual meeting, the Descendants of American Farmers will host online events throughout the year where members learn about various aspects of farming.

Most lineage societies have some type of publication. These serve as a vehicle to let the membership know about the activities of the society. Common items included in these newsletters or magazines are an announcement of upcoming events, a listing of new members, articles of historic interest pertaining to the society, etc.

Membership in a society allows one to purchase the insignia of that society. It may be a simple medallion hanging from a ribbon, or more elaborate. There may be a bar with the ancestor's name engraved on it, or another bar to indicate the chapter or state of membership. Some societies offer pins to show offices or chairmanships held by the member, others have pins to show that certain donations have been made. The wearing of insignia is optional, but many active members choose to do so.

Figure 9.2 – Examples of insignia that commonly include a bar for the chapter and a bar for the ancestor. Additional pins for service, awards, etc. may be available. At the bottom is a branch bar containing insignia for several societies.

Supplemental Applications

If a member has more than one qualifying ancestor, they may wish to file a supplemental application. The documentation process is similar to their original application. It is usually not necessary to provide documentation for the generations that are the same as those proven on the original application, but be sure to include documentation of the link from the previously proven application to the new lineage.

The Guild of Colonial Artisans and Tradesmen bestows a special recognition for members who have proven an ancestor in each of their six "minor" guilds. These members are known as "Master Guilders."

CHAPTER 10

SPECIAL CONSIDERATIONS

Non-Direct Lineages

Most lineage societies rely on direct lineage from the applicant to the qualifying ancestor; in other words, the ancestor is a grandparent, great-grandparent, and so on.

Some societies allow collateral descent as well. The qualifying ancestor may be a sibling of a direct ancestor; in other words, an aunt or uncle, great-aunt or great-uncle, etc. A common reason for a society to allow collateral descent would be that few descendants came from that sibling. Some of the Civil War societies allow this because so many qualifying ancestors died before having children of their own. It is a way to honor these young men and women.

A few societies allow a connection to a famous cousin. It is not necessary to descend directly from this famous person but to share a common ancestor. The Presidents and First Ladies society is like this. Members may be related to the President or First Lady (known as propositi) through an ancestor several generations distant, making them cousins of varying degrees and removals.

Very few societies allow adoptive lineages to qualify. One of these is the Daughters of Utah Pioneers. If an adoptee wishes to join most lineal societies, they would need to establish their lineage through their biological parent. Some of the larger societies are beginning to consider the use of DNA as evidence, but always in conjunction with documentary evidence.

The lineages below should begin with the Common Ancestor (from Page 1) and continue down to your President or First Lady (in the left column) and to you (in the right column). NOTE that the Common Ancestor is already in the appropriate place for both lineages.

Non-First Lady Presidential Wife's Lineage	**Applicant's Lineage**

Figure 10.1 – An example of an application used to prove "cousinship" to a famous person.

Societies for Children

Some lineage societies are solely for younger members, and some include members of all ages. The most well-known of the children's societies is the Children of the American Revolution. Members can join as soon as they have a birth certificate and remain a member until their twenty-second birthday. Young members hold office and run meetings with the guidance of adults from the parent organizations: the Daughters of the American Revolution, the Sons of the American Revolution, and the Sons of the Revolution. Similarly, the Children of the American Colonists has adult mentors from the Daughters of the American Colonists and the Sons of American Colonists.

These societies provide the opportunity for the younger generation to get involved in community service, patriotism, and historic preservation just like the societies for adults. In addition, children gain experience with public speaking and parliamentary procedure.

Figure 10.2 – A Children of the American Colonists member reporting at an annual meeting.

Some societies have members of all ages, with children constituting "junior" members. The Daughters of 1812 has both boys and girls up to age eighteen who will participate with their adult members. New England Women offers junior membership to girls aged six to eighteen, and cradle roll membership to boys and girls from birth to age six. In addition to mentoring the Children of the American Revolution, the Sons of the American Revolution allows boys of any age to join their ranks.

Non-lineage memberships

While members of a lineage society are, by definition, lineally descended from a qualifying ancestor, some societies have another category of membership for non-related persons.

The Founders of Norwich originally began as a lineage society but has evolved into a historic organization that welcomes anyone as a supporter. They have a distinct category for members by descent.

The Descendants of Whaling Masters has different categories of membership depending on whether the ancestor was a whaling master or part of a whaling crew. They allow collateral membership as well as associate membership for non-descendants.

Certificate Only Societies

Some lineage societies do not have meetings or dues. Essentially, they only offer a certificate, and occasionally some type of insignia. The benefit of applying to one of these is to honor your ancestor and have your research approved by another person. The application process is usually similar to that of a regular lineage society, but the application fee is much less. They often are offered through a state or local genealogical society. The Prairie Pioneer and Prairie Patriot programs of the Illinois Genealogical Society are some examples. The sponsoring genealogical society may require membership prior to applying for a certificate, as with First Families of Ohio.

Old World Societies

Some societies honor Royal or other "old world" ancestors. Many of these are by invitation only and therefore not discussed further. They may require documentation of as many as forty generations (or more). So-called "gateway ancestors" can be used for membership. These are colonial and early American immigrants with well-documented Royal lineage. They are usually listed on the society's webpage. Once the applicant has documented their lineage to the gateway ancestor, the remainder of the lineage can usually be found in a published lineage book.

APPENDIX – SELECTED SOCIETY LISTING

This list is not exhaustive but gives more information about some of the societies mentioned in this book. If you are interested in any of these societies, see the listed website for specific details and further information about each.

Associated Daughters of Early American Witches - https://www.adeaw.us/ - women who descend from someone who was suspected, accused, or tried for witchcraft in Colonial America before 1700. Meets annually in April.

Continental Society Daughters of Indian Wars - https://csdiw.org/ - women who descend from someone who participated in any activity (friendly or hostile) with a Native American between 1607 – 1900, or who is a descendant of a Native American. Chapters in several states.

Dames of the Loyal Legion of the United States of America – http://dollus.org – women who descend from an officer in the Union Army during the Civil War. Direct and collateral descent accepted. Chapters in several states.

Descendants of American Prisoners of War – https://dapow.weebly.com - men and women who descend from individuals who were a prisoner of war from 1607 through the present day. Direct and collateral descent accepted. Meets annually in April.

Descendants of Cape Cod and the Islands – https://desccapecodandislands.weebly.com – men and women who descend from individuals who owned land, resided, or conducted business on Cape Cod, Nantucket or Martha's Vineyard prior to 31 December 1699. Meets annually in October.

Descendants of Colonial Regulators - https://colonialregulators.weebly.com/ - men and women who descend from individuals involved in the Regulation movement prior to 1777. Direct and collateral descent accepted. Meets annually in April.

Descendants of Early American Governors, 1607-1860 – https://earlygovernors.org – Men and women who descend from an ancestor who served as a Governor or Assistant/Lieutenant Governor of an area within the boundaries of present-day United States of America. Meets virtually with biennial site visits.

Descendants of Early Postmasters 1607-1900 - https://descendantsof earlypostmasters.weebly.com/ - men and women who descend from anyone who aided in the American postal system. Meets annually in April.

Descendants of Fossors – https://fossors.org – Men and women who descend from someone who assisted in death and burial between 1607 and 1860. Examples include ancestors who worked as a gravedigger, coroner, undertaker or donated land for a cemetery. Meets biennially in April.

Descendants of the Founders of Ancient Windsor – https://dfaw.org – men and women who descend from the first settlers of Windsor, Connecticut. Meets annually.

Descendants of Founders of New Jersey – https://njfounders.org – Men and women who descend from a founder of New Jersey prior to 17 April 1702. Meets twice yearly in a historic location.

Descendants of Whaling Masters – https://whalingmasters.org – Descendants of whaling masters or their crew. Allows collateral membership and associate membership. Meets annually.

First Families of Ohio – https://ogs.org/about/lineage/ffo - Members of the Ohio Genealogical Society who are direct descendants of individuals who settled in the State of Ohio prior to 1821. Certificate only society.

Flagon and Trencher: Descendants of Colonial Tavern Keepers – https:// flagonandtrencher.org - Men and women who descend from an ancestor who conducted a tavern or inn located in one of the original thirteen colonies before the Revolutionary War. Meets annually at a colonial tavern.

General Society of the War of 1812 – https://gswar1812.org – Men who descend from an individual who rendered military service between 7 November 1811 and 18 July 1815. Member societies in several states.

General Society of Mayflower Descendants – https://themayflowersociety .org – Men and women who descend from a passenger on the *Mayflower*. Member Societies in every state.

General Society Sons of the Revolution – https://sr1776.org – men and boys who descend from a military ancestor who fought in the American Revolution. Member societies in several states.

Guild of Colonial Artisans and Tradesmen 1607-1783 - https://guildcolonialartsandtrades.weebly.com/ - men and women who descend from an artisan or tradesman who lived in the American colonies between 1607 and 1783. Qualifying ancestors are in one of six "minor guild" categories and members who prove an ancestor in each category are known as Master Guilders. Meets annually in April.

Hereditary Order of the Families of the Presidents and First Ladies of America – https://presidentsandfirstladies.org – Men and women who have a blood relationship to any President or First Lady of the United States. Meets annually in April.

Hereditary Order of the Red Dragon - https://www.facebook.com/p/Hereditary-Order-of-the-Red-Dragon-100064320687073- men and women who descend from ancient Welsh Kings or a verified Welsh immigrant to America prior to 1776. Meets annually in April.

International Society Daughters of Utah Pioneers – http://www.dupinternational.org/ - women who directly descend from someone who settled in Utah prior to 1869. Companies (chapters) in several states.

Jamestowne Society – https://jamestowne.org – men and women who descend from early settlers in Jamestowne, Virginia prior to 1700 or persons who invested in its establishment. Companies (chapters) in several states.

Military Order of the Southern Cross in the Pacific Theater – https://moscpt.org – men and women who descend from an American Serviceperson in the Pacific Theater of World War II between 7 December 1941 and 2 September 1951. Meets annually online.

National Guild of St. Margaret of Scotland – https://guildofstmargaret.com – men and women who descend from St. Margaret of Scotland. Meets annually in April.

National Huguenot Society - https://nationalhuguenotsociety.org/ - men and women who descend from Huguenots (French Protestants) who escaped religious persecution in France. Chapters in several states.

National Society Children of American Colonists – https://nsdac.org/nscac - children who descend from an American colonist who served in one of 27 capacities prior to July 4, 1776. Chapters in several states.

National Society Children of American Revolution – https://www.nscar.org – children who descend from a patriot of the American Revolution. Societies (chapters) in several states.

National Society Colonial Dames of the Seventeenth Century - https://www.colonialdames17c.org/ - women who descend from an ancestor who served in an original colony prior to 1701. Local chapters in several states.

National Society Colonial Daughters of the Seventeenth Century - https://www.colonialdaughters17th.org/ - women who descend from settlers who rendered distinguished service prior to 1700. Chapters in several states.

National Society Dames of the Court of Honor – http://nsdch.org – Women 16 and over who descend from a commissioned officer who served from 1607 through 1865, or from a colonial Governor. Chapters in several states.

National Society Daughters of American Colonists - https://nsdac.org/ - women who descend from American colonists who served in one of 27 capacities prior to July 4, 1776. Local chapters in several states.

National Society Daughters of the American Revolution – http://www.dar.org – women who descend from a patriot (military and non-military) of the American Revolution. Local chapters in several states and overseas.

National Society Daughters of Colonial Wars – https://nsdcw.org – women who descend from an ancestor who served in a military or high civil position prior to April 19, 1775. Chapters in several states.

National Society Daughters of Founders and Patriots of America - https://www.nationalsocietydfpa.com/ - women who can establish an unbroken paternal line, from either their father or mother, back to a founder who arrived prior to 1687 with an intermediate patriot of the Revolutionary War. Chapters in several states.

National Society Daughters of the Union 1861-1865 - https://www.nsdu.org/ - women who descend from someone who rendered military or civil service to the Union during the Civil War. Collateral lineage accepted. Chapters in several states.

National Society Descendants of American Farmers - https://www.nsdoaf.com/ - men, women, and children who descend from a farmer in the

United States between 1776 and 1914. Meets annually along with frequent online events.

National Society Descendants of Colonial Indentured Servants – http:// indenturedservants.org – men and women who descend from an indentured servant. Meets annually in April.

National Society Descendants of Early Quakers - http://www.earlyquakers.org/ - men, women, and children who descend from a member of the Society of Friends prior to 1835. Meets annually in April.

National Society of Descendants of Textile Workers of America - http://www.textileworker.com/ - men and women who descend from anyone engaged in textile manufacture. Meets annually.

National Society Sons and Daughters of the Pilgrims – https://societyofthepilgrims.com - men and women who descend from any immigrant who settled before 1700 in the area of the current United States. Branches (chapters) in several states.

National Society Sons of the American Colonists – https://american colonists.org – Men who descend from an ancestor who rendered civil or military service in the colonies prior to 4 July 1776. Chapters in several states.

National Society Sons of the American Revolution – https://www.sar.org – men and boys who descend from a patriot of the American Revolution. Local chapters in several states.

National Society New England Women – https://newenglandwomen.org – women who descend from anyone born in New England before 1789. Colonies (chapters) in several states.

National Society Southern Dames of America - http://southerndames ofamerica.com/ - women with southern ancestry. Chapters in several states.

National Society United States Daughters of 1812 - https://usdaughters 1812.org/ - women and children who descend from someone who rendered civil or military service during 1784-1815. Local chapters in several states.

National Society Women Descendants of the Ancient and Honorable Artillery Company - http://www.wdahac.com/ - women who descend from colonial members of the Ancient and Honorable Artillery Company in Boston. Courts (chapters) in several states.

Order of First Families of New Hampshire – http://firstfamiliesofnew hampshire.org – men and women whose ancestors resided in or owned land or businesses in New Hampshire between 1622 and 1680. Meets annually in April.

Prairie Patriots – https://ilgensoc.org/cpage.php?pt559 – men and women who descend from veterans of the Revolutionary War through World War II who lived in Illinois. Collateral lineages accepted. Certificate only society.

Prairie Pioneers -https://ilgensoc.org/cpage.php?pt559 – men and women who descend from a resident of Illinois before 1880. Certificate only society.

Presidential Families of America – http://presidentialfamilies.org – men and women who have a blood relationship to a United States President. Meets annually in April.

Society of the Descendants of the Colonial Clergy - https://www. colonialclergy.com/ - men and women who descend from an ordained clergyman prior to 1776. Meets annually.

Society of the Descendants of Lady Godiva - https://societyof descendantsofladygodiva.weebly.com/ - men and women who descend from Lady Godiva (980-1067 AD). Meets annually in April.

Society of the Founders of Norwich – https://leffingwellhousemuseum.org – Men and women who descend from the 35 founders of Norwich, Connecticut. Allows non-descendants to join as supporters.

Sons and Daughters of the United States Middle Passage – https://sdusmp.org – Men and women of African descent whose ancestor was forced into slavery prior to December 1865. Meets annually with scholarly presentations.

United Daughters of the Confederacy - https://hqudc.org/ - women who descend from someone who served in the military or gave material aid to the Confederate States of America. Collateral lineages accepted. Chapters in several states.

United Empire Loyalist Association of Canada - https://uelac.ca/ - descendants of a proven Loyalist during the American Revolution. Branches (chapters) in several Canadian Provinces. Offers both lineage and non-lineage memberships.

SELECTED BIBLIOGRAPHY

Research Techniques

Greenwood, Val D. *The Researcher's Guide to American Genealogy.* Fourth edition. Baltimore: Genealogical Publishing Company, 2017.
A comprehensive guide for genealogical research in the United States.

Hatcher, Patricia Law. *Locating Your Roots: Discover Your Ancestors Using Land Records.* Baltimore: Genealogical Publishing Company, 2016.
How to locate and use land records and maps.

Mills, Elizabeth Shown. *Evidence Explained: Citing History Sources from Artifacts to Cyberspace.* Fourth edition. Baltimore: Genealogical Publishing Company, 2024.
This is the "go-to" source for genealogical citations.

Morton, Sunny Jane and Henderson, Harold A. *How to Find Your Family History in U.S. Church Records: A Genealogist's Guide.* Baltimore: Genealogical Publishing company, 2019.
Information on finding and using church records, with specifics for several denominations.

Rose, Christine. *Courthouse Research for Family Historians: Your Guide to Genealogical Treasures.* San Jose: CR Publications, 2004.
Information on the appropriate courthouse office, using the index, and some of the obscure words encountered in courthouse records.

Rose, Christine. *Military Bounty Land: 1776-1855.* San Jose: CR Publications, 2011.
Guide to finding bounty land records and getting the most information from them.

Suggested sources for "service"

Anderson, Robert Charles. *The Great Migration Begins* and *The Great Migration.* Boston: New England Historic Genealogical Society, 1995-2011.
Two multi-volume works with in-depth information on immigrants to New England between 1620-1635. These references are invaluable to anyone with early New England Ancestry and provide information on occupations and public service as well as residency.

Arnold, Lisa Parry. *Thee & Me: A Beginner's Guide to Early Quaker Records.* n.p., 2014.
Introduction to the Quaker religion and their records.

Bockstruck, Lloyd deWitt. *Revolutionary War Pensions Awarded by State Governments 1775-1874, the General and Federal Governments Prior to 1814, and by Private Acts of Congress to 1905.* Baltimore: Genealogical Publishing Company, 2011.
Extensive listing of Revolutionary War Pensioners.

Colket, Meredith B. Jr. *Founders of Early American Families: Emigrants from Europe 1607-1657.* Revised edition. Cleveland: Order of Founders and Patriots of America, 1985.
A listing of ancestors proven by members of the Order of Founders and Patriots of America with brief information about each.

Dorman, John Frederick. *Adventurers of Purse and Person Virginia 1607-1624/5.* Fourth edition. Three volumes. Baltimore: Genealogical Publishing Company, var.
Genealogical information on Virginia Company members and their descendants.

Faris, David. *Plantagenet Ancestry of Seventeenth-Century Colonists: The Descent from the Later Plantagenet Kings of England, Henry III, Edward I, and Edward III, of Emigrants from England and Wales to the North American Colonies before 1701.* Second edition. Boston: New England Historic Genealogical Society, 1999.
Royal descents of several Plantagenet Kings to "Gateway" ancestors.

Grundset, Eric G. *Connecticut in the American Revolution: A Source Guide for Genealogists and Historians.* Washington: National Society Daughters of the American Revolution, 2016.
Extensive Bibliography of sources containing information about Revolutionary War service. Similar guides exist for other colonies.

Hudgins, Dennis Ray. *Cavaliers and Pioneers: Abstracts of Virginia Land Patents and Grants.* Richmond: Virginia Genealogical Society, var.
Multi-volume set containing abstracts of early Virginia land records through the Revolutionary War.

Johnson, Eric Eugene and Jacks, Thomas E. *Roster of Members and Their Ancestors of the General Society of the War of 1812.* Bicentennial edition. Baltimore: Otter Bay Books, 2017.
A listing of ancestors proven by members of the General Society War of 1812.

Kallal, Jeannine Sheldon. *Genealogical Data of the Ancient & Honorable Artillery Company of Massachusetts, 1638-1774.* Revised edition. n.p.: National Society Women Descendants of the Ancient & Honorable Artillery Company of Massachusetts, 2020.
A listing of over 1200 members of the early Boston-area military company with genealogical information.

Kallal, Jeannine Sheldon. *Register of Qualified Huguenot Ancestors of the National Huguenot Society.* Fifth edition. San Antonio: National Huguenot Society, 2012.
A listing of Huguenot (persecuted French Protestant) ancestors with genealogical information.

Mayflower Society. *Mayflower Families Through Five Generations.* Also known as the "Silver Books".
Several volumes tracing five (or more) generations from Mayflower ancestors.

Nagy, Kimberly Ormsby. *Associated Daughters of Early American Witches Roll of Ancestors.* Second edition. Berwyn Heights, MD: Heritage Books, 2022.
Listing of over 300 ancestors who were suspected, accused or executed for witchcraft prior to 1700, many with 2-3 generations of genealogical information.

Ogden, Evelyn Hunt. *Founders of New Jersey: First Settlements, Colonists and Biographies by Descendants*. Third edition. n.p., 2016.
Compiled biographies of Early New Jersey settlers.

Richardson, Douglas, *Royal Ancestry: A Study in Colonial and Medieval Families.* 5 volumes, Salt Lake City: 2013.
A thorough reference for Royal lineages.

Roberts, Gary Boyd. *Ancestors of American Presidents.* Santa Clarita: Carl Boyer, 1995.
Lineages of American Presidents through Clinton along with lineages of some First Ladies.

Roberts, Gary Boyd. *The Royal Descents of 900 Immigrants to the American Colonies, Quebec or the United States Who Were Themselves Notable or Left Descendants Notable in American History.* Second edition. Baltimore: Genealogical Publishing Company, 2022.
The most comprehensive listing of "Gateway" ancestors for royal and medieval lineages.

Williams, Alicia Crane. *Early New England Families 1641-1700.* Boston: New England Historic Genealogical Society, 2015-2019.
In-depth information on several prominent New England Colonists who arrived after the Great Migration.

www.ingramcontent.com/pod-product-compliance
Lightning Source LLC
Chambersburg PA
CBHW072211270326
41930CB00011B/2611

* 9 7 8 0 8 0 6 3 2 1 3 9 4 *